The PRIMARY SOURCE

Historical Documents:
The Founding Period

by

Julia Hargrove

Volume Two

ABOUT THE AUTHOR

JULIA HARGROVE was born in San Francisco,
California, and grew up in Colorado Springs,
Colorado. She received her B.A. degree in History
and English from Western State College,
Gunnison, Colorado, in 1969, and her M.A. degree
in American History from the University of
Texas at Austin in 1970. She has been a teacher
at Doherty High School in Colorado Springs since
1976 and has used much of the material in this
series in her American history classes.

Copyright 1987. The Perfection Form Company,
Logan, Iowa 51546

TABLE OF CONTENTS

INTRODUCTION

Effective history teaching goes beyond the information presented in a textbook. To bring history alive for students, the teacher needs to enrich the history curriculum with materials that will hold the students' interest while at the same time giving them a different perspective on their historical studies.

The Primary Source is designed to help fill this need. In this series students go beyond the textbook to read original documents from American history. In the process, they learn firsthand about the people and events described in their textbooks. At the same time, they get experience with one of the historian's key tasks: analyzing and interpreting primary source material.

Each volume of *The Primary Source* presents a different series of historical documents. Each document is accompanied by a study guide containing two sets of questions. The first set, **Facts and Concepts**, asks students to critically examine and analyze the important ideas in the document. The second set, **For Further Understanding**, takes the students outside the document to solve historical and practical problems.

Each volume is fully reproducible, enabling the teacher to give each student his or her own copy of a document and its study guide. An answer key for the teacher is included at the end of each volume.

In Volume 2 students are introduced to historical documents of the founding period. These documents provide new insights into the establishment of American government, and show students the background of the institutions that have governed the U.S. for more than two hundred years.

ALBANY PLAN OF UNION

1754

The Albany Congress of 1754 proposed this plan to unite the colonies. The plan involved establishing a Grand Council, made up of representatives from all of the colonies, to make laws for the colonies. It also proposed creating a president-general to act as chief executive. The Albany Plan contained many ideas that later appeared in the U.S. Constitution.

It is proposed that humble application be made for an act of Parliament of Great Britain, by virtue of which one general government may be formed in America, including all the said colonies, within and under which government each colony may retain its present constitution, except in the particulars wherein a change may be directed by the said act, as hereafter follows.

1. That the said general government be administered by a President-General, to be appointed and supported by the crown; and a Grand Council, to be chosen by the representatives of the people of the several Colonies met in their respective assemblies.

2. That within _____ months after the passing such act, the House of Representatives that happen to be sitting within that time, or that shall be especially for that purpose convened, may and shall choose members for the Grand Council, in the following proportion, that is to say,

Massachusetts Bay	7
New Hampshire	2
Connecticut	5
Rhode Island	2
New York	4
New Jersey	3
Pennsylvania	6
Maryland	4
Virginia	7

North Carolina	4
South Carolina	4
	48

3. _____ who shall meet for the first time at the city of Philadelphia, being called by the President-General as soon as conveniently may be after his appointment.

4. That there shall be a new election of the members of the Grand Council every three years; and, on the death or resignation of any member, his place should be supplied by a new choice at the next sitting of the Assembly of the Colony he represented.

5. That after the first three years, when the proportion of money arising out of each Colony to the general treasury can be known, the number of members to be chosen for each Colony shall, from time to time, in all ensuing elections, be regulated by that proportion, yet so as that the number to be chosen by any one Province be not more than seven, nor less than two.

6. That the Grand Council shall meet once in every year, and oftener if occasion require, at such time and place as they shall adjourn to at the last preceding meeting, or as they shall be called to meet at by the President-General on any emergency; he having first obtained in writing the consent of seven of the members to such call, and sent duly and timely notice to the whole.

7. That the Grand Council have power to choose their speaker; and shall neither be dissolved, prorogued, nor continued sitting longer than six weeks at one time, without their own consent or the special command of the crown.

8. That the members of the

Grand Council shall be allowed for their service ten shillings sterling per diem, during their session and journey to and from the place of meeting; twenty miles to be reckoned a day's journey.

9. That the assent of the President-General be requisite to all acts of the Grand Council, and that it be his office and duty to cause them to be carried into execution.

10. That the President-General, with the advice of the Grand Council, hold or direct all Indian treaties, in which the general interest of the Colonies may be concerned; and make peace or declare war with Indian nations.

11. That they make such laws as they judge necessary for regulating all Indian trade.

12. That they make all purchases from Indians, for the crown, of lands not now within the bounds of particular Colonies, or that shall not be within their bounds when some of them are reduced to more convenient dimensions.

13. That they make new settlements on such purchases, by granting lands in the King's name, reserving a quitrent to the crown for the use of the general treasury.

14. That they make laws for regulating and governing such new settlements, till the crown shall think fit to form them into particular governments.

15. That they raise and pay soldiers and build forts for the defence of any of the Colonies, and equip vessels of force to guard the coasts and protect the trade on the ocean, lakes, or great rivers; but they shall not impress men in any Colony, without the consent of the Legislature.

16. That for these purposes they have power to make laws, and lay and levy such general duties, imposts, or taxes, as to them shall appear most equal and just (considering the ability and other circumstances of the inhabitants in the several Colonies), and such as may be collected with the least inconvenience to the people; rather discouraging luxury, than loading industry with unnecessary burdens.

17. That they may appoint a General Treasurer and Particular Treasurer in each government when necessary; and, from time to time, may order the sums in the treasuries of each government into the general treasury; or draw on them for special payments, as they find most convenient.

18. Yet no money to issue but by joint orders of the President-General and Grand Council; except where sums have been appropriated to particular purposes, and the President-General is previously empowered by an act to draw such sums.

19. That the general accounts shall be yearly settled and reported to the several Assemblies.

20. That a quorum of the Grand Council, empowered to act with the President-General, do consist of twenty-five members; among whom there shall be one or more from a majority of the Colonies.

21. That the laws made by them for the purposes aforesaid shall not be repugnant, but, as near as may be, agreeable to the laws of England, and shall be transmitted to the King in Council for approbation, as soon as may be after their passing; and if not disapproved within three years after presentation, to remain in force.

22. That, in case of the death of the President-General, the Speaker of the Grand Council for

the time being shall succeed, and be vested with the same powers and authorities, to continue till the King's pleasure be known.

23. That all military commission officers, whether for land or sea service, to act under this general constitution, shall be nominated by the President-General; but the approbation of the Grand Council is to be obtained, before they receive their commissions. And all civil officers are to be nominated by the Grand Council, and to receive the President-General's approbation before they officiate.

24. But, in case of vacancy by death or removal of any officer, civil or military, under this constitution, the Governor of the Province in which such vacancy happens may appoint, till the pleasure of the President-General and Grand Council can be known.

25. That the particular military as well as civil establishments in each Colony remain in their present state, the general constitution notwithstanding; and that on sudden emergencies any Colony may defend itself, and lay the accounts of expense thence arising before the President-General and General Council, who may allow and order payment of the same, as far as they judge such accounts just and reasonable.

ALBANY PLAN OF UNION

1754

I. Facts and Concepts

1. According to the introductory paragraph, what is the purpose of this document?

   _____

   _____

2. Quote a phrase from the introductory paragraph that tells the colonies that the new plan will not interfere with their internal affairs.

   _____

   _____

3. Read Section 1 and answer the following questions.

   a. How is the president-general to be chosen?

   _____

   b. How are the representatives to the Grand Council to be chosen?

   _____

   _____

4. According to Section 4, what is the length of a term of office on the Grand Council?

   _____

5. Read Section 5 and answer the following questions.

   a. How is the number of representatives each colony sends to the Grand Council to be decided after the first three years the government is in effect?

   _____

   _____

b. Do you think this is a fair proposal? Why or why not?

_____

_____

_____

_____

6. Read Section 6 and answer the following questions.

   a. How often is the Grand Council supposed to meet in regular session?

   _____

   b. Who or what body has the power to call an emergency meeting of the Grand Council?

   _____

7. Read Section 7 and answer the following questions.

   a. Look up the word "prorogue" in a dictionary or history book and write down its meaning.

   _____

   b. What three things cannot be done to the Grand Council without its consent or a special command of the king or queen?

   _____

   _____

8. Read Section 9 and answer the following questions.

   a. In your own words, explain the meaning of the phrase "the assent of the President-General be requisite to all acts of the Grand Council."

   _____

   _____

   _____

b. What is the main duty of the president-general?

_____

_____

9. Sections 10, 11, and 12 give the Grand Council the power
   to do what five things in regard to Indians?

_____

_____

_____

_____

_____

10. Read Section 15 and answer the following questions.

   a. What two military branches is the Grand Council allowed
      to create and support?

_____

   b. Look up the word "impress" and write down its military
      meaning.

_____

11. What two powers does Section 16 give to the Grand
    Council?

_____

12. What does the phrase "each government" in Section 17
    refer to?

_____

13. Read Section 20 and answer the following questions.

   a. Look up "quorum" and write down its meaning.

_____

   b. What number of representatives constitutes a quorum in
      the Grand Council?

_____

14. Read Section 21 and answer the following questions.

    a. The laws of the colonial government must agree with the laws of what other country?

_____

    b. Who has the final power to approve or disapprove of the laws passed by the Grand Council?

_____

15. Look back over the document and describe the three-step process by which a bill would become a law in the colonies.

_____

_____

_____

II. For Further Understanding

16. Who wrote the Albany Plan of Union?

_____

17. What events of 1754 led the members of the Albany Congress to believe that a plan of union was necessary?

_____

_____

_____

18. What happened to the Albany Plan? Why?

_____

_____

_____

19. Which of the three branches of today's U.S. government is not included in the Albany Plan?

_____

20. Section 22 provides that the Speaker of the Grand Council should succeed the president-general if the latter died. Who are the first five people in line to succeed the president of the U.S. now if he or she should die?

1. _____

2. _____

3. _____

4. _____

5. _____

DECLARATION AND RESOLVES OF THE FIRST CONTINENTAL CONGRESS

1774

After the British Parliament passed a series of laws against the colonies, especially Massachusetts, the colonists decided that they needed a unified organization. They formed the First Continental Congress to register their discontent with British policies and discuss courses of action. This document came out of the meeting of the First Continental Congress in Philadelphia in 1774.

Whereas, since the close of the last war, the British parliament, claiming a power of right to bind the people of America by statute in all cases whatsoever, hath, in some acts expressly imposed taxes on them, and in others, under various pretences, but in fact for the purpose of raising a revenue, hath imposed rates and duties payable in these colonies, established a board of commissioners with unconstitutional powers, and extended the jurisdiction of courts of Admiralty not only for collecting the said duties, but for the trial of causes merely arising within the body of a county.

And whereas, in consequence of other statutes, judges who before held only estates at will in their offices, have been made dependent on the Crown alone for their salaries, and standing armies kept in times of peace. And it has lately been resolved in Parliament, that by force of a statute made in the thirty-fifth year of the reign of king Henry the Eighth, colonists may be transported to England, and tried there upon accusations for treasons and misprisions, or concealments of treasons committed in the colonies; and by a late statute, such trials have been directed in cases therein mentioned.

And whereas, in the last session of Parliament, [four] statutes were made . . . , All which statutes are impolitic, unjust, and cruel, as well as unconstitutional, and most dangerous and destructive of American rights.

And whereas, Assemblies have been frequently dissolved, contrary to the rights of the people, when they attempted to deliberate on grievances; and their dutiful, humble, loyal, & reasonable petitions to the crown for redress, have been repeatedly treated with contempt, by His Majesty's ministers of state:

The good people of the several Colonies of New-hampshire, Massachusetts-bay, Rhode-island and Providence plantations, Connecticut, New-York, New-Jersey, Pennsylvania, Newcastle Kent and Sussex on Delaware, Maryland, Virginia, North-Carolina, and South-Carolina, justly alarmed at these arbitrary proceedings of parliament and administration, have severally elected, constituted, and appointed deputies to meet, and sit in general Congress, in the city of Philadelphia, in order to obtain such establishment, as that their religion, laws, and liberties, may not be subverted:

Whereupon the deputies so appointed being now assembled, in a full and free representation of these Colonies, taking into their most serious consideration the best means of attaining the ends aforesaid, do in the first place, as Englishmen their ancestors in like cases have usually done, for asserting and vindicating their rights and liberties, declare,

That the inhabitants of the English Colonies in North America, by the immutable laws of nature, the principles of the English constitution, and the several charters or compacts, have the following Rights:

Resolved, N. C. D.

1. That they are entitled to life, liberty, and property, & they have never ceded to any sovereign power whatever, a right to dispose of either without their consent.

2. That our ancestors, who first settled these colonies, were at the time of their emigration from the mother country, entitled to all the rights, liberties, and immunities of free and natural-born subjects within the realm of England.

3. That by such emigration they by no means forfeited, surrendered, or lost any of those rights, but that they were, and their descendants now are entitled to the exercise and enjoyment of all such of them, as their local and other circumstances enable them to exercise and enjoy.

4. That the foundation of English liberty, and of all free government, is a right in the people to participate in their legislative council: and as the English colonists are not represented, and from their local and other circumstances, cannot properly be represented in the British parliament, they are entitled to a free and exclusive power of legislation in their several provincial legislatures, where their right of representation can alone be preserved, in all cases of taxation and internal polity, subject only to the negative of their sovereign, in such manner as has been heretofore used and accustomed. But, from the necessity of the case, and a regard to the mutual interest of both countries, we cheerfully consent to the operation of such acts of the British parliament, as are bona fide restrained to the regulation of our external commerce, for the purpose of securing the commercial advantages of the whole empire to the mother country, and the commercial benefits of its respective members excluding every idea of taxation, internal or external, for raising a revenue on the subjects in America without their consent.

5. That the respective colonies are entitled to the common law of England, and more especially to the great and inestimable privilege of being tried by their peers of the vicinage, according to the course of that law.

6. That they are entitled to the benefit of such of the English statutes, as existed at the time of their colonization; and which they have, by experience, respectively found to be applicable to their several local and other circumstances.

7. That these, his majesty's colonies, are likewise entitled to all the immunities and privileges granted and confirmed to them by royal charters, or secured by their several codes of provincial laws.

8. That they have a right peaceably to assemble, consider of their grievances, and petition the King; and that all prosecutions, prohibitory proclamations, and commitments for the same, are illegal.

9. That the keeping a Standing army in these colonies, in times of peace, without the consent of the legislature of that colony in which such army is kept, is against law.

10. It is indispensably necessary to good government, and rendered essential by the English constitution, that the constituent branches of the legislature

be independent of each other; that, therefore, the exercise of legislative power in several colonies, by a council appointed during pleasure, by the crown, is unconstitutional, dangerous, and destructive to the freedom of American legislation.

All and each of which the aforesaid deputies, in behalf of themselves, and their constituents, do claim, demand, and insist on, as their indubitable rights and liberties; which cannot be legally taken from them, altered or abridged by any power whatever, without their own consent, by their representatives in their several provincial legislatures.

In the course of our inquiry, we find many infringments and violations of the foregoing rights, which, from an ardent desire that harmony and mutual intercourse of affection and interest may be restored, we pass over for the present, and proceed to state such acts and measures as have been adopted since the last war, which demonstrate a system formed to enslave America.

Resolved, That the following acts of Parliament are infringements and violations of the rights of the colonists; and that the repeal of them is essentially necessary, in order to restore harmony between Great Britain and the American colonies, . . . viz.:

The several Acts of 4 Geo. 3, ch. 15 & ch. 34; 5 Geo. 3, ch. 25; 6 Geo. 3, ch. 52; 7 Geo. 3, ch. 41 & 46; 8 Geo. 3, ch. 22; which impose duties for the purpose of raising a revenue in America, extend the powers of the admiralty courts beyond their ancient limits, deprive the American subject of trial by jury, authorize the judges' certificate to indemnify the prosecutor from damages that he might otherwise be liable to,

requiring oppressive security from a claimant of ships and goods seized before he shall be allowed to defend his property; and are subversive of American rights.

Also the 12 Geo. 3, ch. 24, entitled "An act for the better preserving his Majesty's dock-yards, magazines, ships, ammunition, and stores," which declares a new offense in America, and deprives the American subject of a constitutional trial by jury of the vicinage, by authorizing the trial of any person charged with the committing any offense described in the said act, out of the realm, to be indicted and tried for the same in any shire or county within the realm.

Also the three acts passed in the last session of parliament, for stopping the port and blocking up the harbour of Boston, for altering the charter & government of the Massachusetts-bay, and that which is entitled "An Act for the better administration of Justice," &c.

Also the act passed the same session for establishing the Roman Catholick Religion in the province of Quebec, abolishing the equitable system of English laws, and erecting a tyranny there, to the great danger, from so great a dissimilarity of Religion, law, and government, of the neighbouring British colonies . . .

Also the act passed the same session for the better providing suitable quarters for officers and soldiers in his Majesty's service in North America.

Also, that the keeping a standing army in several of these colonies, in time of peace, without the consent of the legislature of that colony in which the army is kept, is against law.

To these grievous acts and measures Americans cannot

submit, but in hopes that their fellow subjects in Great-Britain will, on a revision of them, restore us to that state in which both countries found happiness and prosperity, we have for the present only resolved to pursue the following peaceable measures: 1st. To enter into a nonimportation, non-consumption, and nonexportation agreement or association.

2. To prepare an address to the people of Great Britain, and a memorial to the inhabitants of British America, & 3. To prepare a loyal address to his Majesty, agreeable to resolutions already entered into.

DECLARATION AND RESOLVES OF THE FIRST CONTINENTAL CONGRESS

1774

I. Facts and Concepts

1. In your own words, list five grievances presented by the colonists in the first and second paragraphs of this document.

   _____

   _____

   _____

   _____

   _____

2. What do the colonists protest in the third paragraph?

   _____

   _____

3. What two grievances are listed in the paragraph that begins, "And whereas, Assemblies . . . "?

   _____

   _____

4. According to the paragraph that begins, "The good people . . . ", what had the colonists done to protect their rights?

   _____

5. What three sources of their rights do the colonists list in the paragraph beginning, "That the inhabitants . . . "?

   _____

   _____

   _____

6. What do the colonists claim in Sections 1, 2, and 3 of the paragraph that begins, "Resolved, N. C. D."?

_____

_____

_____

_____

_____

7. Read Section 4 under the paragraph that begins, "Resolved, N. C. D." and answer the following questions.

   a. What basic right is outlined in this section?

   _____

   _____

   b. In what governing body were the colonists not represented, according to this section?

   _____

   c. Since the colonists cannot be represented in this body, what right do they claim?

   _____

   _____

   _____

   d. What control would the king have over colonial laws?

   _____

   _____

   e. What type of laws passed by the British Parliament were the colonists willing to honor?

   _____

   _____

f. The colonists denied that Parliament had the right to pass what types of law without the consent of the colonists?

_____

8. What rights did the colonists claim in Sections 5 through 8 of the paragraph that begins, "Resolved, N. C. D."?

_____

_____

_____

9. Read Section 10 under the paragraph that begins, "Resolved, N. C. D." and answer the following questions.

   a. What condition is described in the first half of this section as necessary to good government?

_____

_____

   b. In what way did the colonists claim the king had violated that condition?

_____

_____

10. Read the paragraph that begins, "All and each of which . . . " and answer the following questions.

   a. What are the "rights and liberties" which the colonists "claim, demand, and insist on" in this paragraph?

_____

_____

   b. What are the only circumstances under which these rights may be taken away from the colonists?

_____

11. In your own words, summarize the resolution of the paragraph that begins, *"Resolved,* that the following . . . "

_____

_____

_____

_____

12. What violations of their rights did the colonists find in the laws named in the paragraph that begins, "The several acts . . . "?

_____

_____

_____

_____

_____

13. Read the paragraph that begins, "Also the 12 Geo. 3, ch. 24, . . . " and answer the following questions.

a. Look up the word "vicinage" in a dictionary and write down its definition.

_____

b. What right did the colonists contend they were being denied in the law mentioned in this paragraph?

_____

_____

14. What three acts by the British do the colonists protest in the paragraph that begins, "Also the three acts . . . "?

_____

_____

_____

15. Read the last paragraph of the document and answer the following questions.

   a. What do the colonists hope the British will do about the laws named in this document?

   _____

   _____

   b. Explain in your own words the three actions the colonists decided to take to protest these laws.

   _____

   _____

   _____

   _____

   _____

II. For Further Understanding

16. The first line of this document contains the phrase "since the close of the last war." What war are the authors talking about?

   _____

17. What name did the colonists give to the group of laws passed by Britain which caused them to convene the First Continental Congress and to write these resolutions?

   _____

18. Who is the "Geo. 3" after whom the laws cited in this document are named?

   _____

19. In the last paragraph of the document, the colonists agree to "enter into a nonimportation, non-consumption, and nonexportation agreement." What one word describes this action?

_____

20. Were the actions taken by the colonists described in this document successful? Explain your answer.

_____

_____

_____

_____

COMMON SENSE

by Thomas Paine

1776

Thomas Paine was one of the strongest colonial advocates of independence from Great Britain. **Common Sense** *clearly and forcefully protested the actions of the king and Parliament. Its simple language and persuasive arguments made many people join the cause for independence.*

In the following pages I offer nothing more than simple facts, plain arguments, and common sense; and have no other preliminaries to settle with the reader, than that he will divest himself of prejudice and prepossession, and suffer his reason and his feelings to determine for themselves; that he will put on, or rather that he will not put off, the true character of a man, and generously enlarge his views beyond the present day.

Volumes have been written on the subject of the struggle between England and America. Men of all ranks have embarked in the controversy, from different motives, and with various designs; but all have been ineffectual, and the period of debate is closed. Arms as the last resource decide the contest; the appeal was the choice of the king, and the continent has accepted the challenge.

The sun never shined on a cause of greater worth. 'Tis not the affair of a city, a county, a province, or a kingdom; but of a continent—of at least one-eighth part of the habitable globe. 'Tis not the concern of a day, a year, or an age; posterity are virtually involved in the contest, and will be more or less affected even to the end of time by the proceedings now. Now is the seedtime of continental union, faith, and honor. The least fracture now will be like a name engraved with the point of a pin on the tender rind of a young oak; the wound would enlarge with the tree, and posterity read it in full grown characters.

By referring the matter from argument to arms, a new era for politics is struck—a new method of thinking has arisen. All plans, proposals, &c. prior to the nineteenth of April, i.e. to the commencement of hostilities, are like the almanacks of the last year; which though proper then, are superseded and useless now. Whatever was advanced by the advocates on either side of the question then, terminated in one and the same point, viz. a union with Great Britain; the only difference between the parties was the method of effecting it; the one proposing force, the other friendship; but it has so far happened that the first has failed, and the second has withdrawn her influence.

As much has been said of the advantages of reconciliation, which, like an agreeable dream, has passed away and left us as we were, it is but right that we should examine the contrary side of the argument, and inquire into some of them any material injuries which these colonies sustain, and always will sustain, by being connected with and dependent on Great Britain. To examine that connection and dependence on the principles of nature and common sense; to see what we have to trust to, if separated, and what we are to expect, if dependent.

I have heard it asserted by some, that as America has flourished under her former connection with Great Britain, the same connection is necessary towards her future happiness, and will always have the same effect. Nothing can be more fallacious than this kind of argument. We may as well assert that because a child has thrived upon milk, that it is never to have meat, or that the first twenty years of our lives is to become a precedent for the next twenty. But even this is admitting more than is true; for I answer roundly that America would have flourished as much, and probably much more, had no European power taken any notice of her. The commerce by which she hath enriched herself are the necessaries of life, and will always have a market while eating is the custom of Europe.

But she has protected us, say some. That she hath engrossed us is true, and defended the continent at our expense as well as her own is admitted; and she would have defended Turkey from the same motive, viz. for the sake of trade and dominion.

Alas! we have been long led away by ancient prejudices and made large sacrifices to superstition. We have boasted the protection of Great Britain without considering that her motive was *interest*, not *attachment;* and that she did not protect us from *our enemies* on *our account,* but from her enemies on her own account, from those who had no quarrel with us on any *other account,* and who will always be our enemies on the *same account.* Let Britain waive her pretensions to the continent, or the continent throw off the dependence, and we should be at peace with France and Spain were they at war with Britain. The miseries of Hanover's last war ought to warn us against connections.

It hath lately been asserted in parliament, that the colonies have no relation to each other but through the parent country, i.e. that Pennsylvania and the Jerseys, and so on for the rest, are sister colonies by the way of England; this is certainly a very roundabout way of proving relationship, but it is the nearest and only true way of proving enmity (or enemyship, if I may so call it). France and Spain never were, nor perhaps ever will be, our enemies as *Americans,* but as our being the *subjects of Great Britain.*

But Britain is the parent country, say some. Then the more shame upon her conduct. Even brutes do not devour their young, nor savages make war upon their families; wherefore, the assertion, if true, turns to her reproach; but it happens not to be true, or only partly so, and the phrase *parent* or *mother country* hath been jesuitically adopted by the king and his parasites, with a low papistical design of gaining an unfair bias on the credulous weakness of our minds. Europe, and not England, is the parent country of America. This new world hath been the asylum for the persecuted lovers of civil and religious liberty from *every part* of Europe. Hither have they fled, not from the tender embraces of the mother, but from the cruelty of the monster; and it is so far true of England, that the same tyranny which drove the first emigrants from home pursues their descendants still.

But, admitting that we were all of English descent, what does it amount to? Nothing. Britain, being now an open enemy, extinguishes every other name and title; and to say that reconciliation is our duty, is truly farcical. The first king of England, of the present line (William the Conqueror) was a Frenchman, and half the peers of England are descendants from the same country; wherefore, by the same method of reasoning,

20

England ought to be governed by France.

Much hath been said of the united strength of Britain and the colonies, that in conjunction they might bid defiance to the world. But this is mere presumption, the fate of war is uncertain; neither do the expressions mean anything, for this continent would never suffer itself to be drained of inhabitants to support the British arms in either Asia, Africa, or Europe.

Besides, what have we to do with setting the world at defiance? Our plan is commerce, and that, well attended to, will secure us the peace and friendship of all Europe; because it is the interest of all Europe to have America a *free port.* Her trade will always be a protection, and her barrenness of gold and silver secure her from invaders.

I challenge the warmest advocate for reconciliation to show a single advantage that this continent can reap, by being connected with Great Britain. I repeat the challenge, not a single advantage is derived. Our corn will fetch its price in any market in Europe, and our imported goods must be paid for, buy them where we will.

TO CONCLUDE. However strange it may appear to some, or however unwilling they may be to think so, matters not, but many strong and striking reasons may be given to show that nothing can settle our affairs so expeditiously as an open and determined DECLARATION FOR INDEPENDENCE. Some of which are:

First. It is the custom of nations, when any two are at war, for some other powers not engaged in the quarrel to step in as mediators, and bring about the preliminaries of a peace; but while America calls herself the Subject of Great Britain, no power, however well disposed she may be, can offer her mediation. Wherefore, in our present state we may quarrel on forever.

Secondly. It is unreasonable to suppose that France or Spain will give us any kind of assistance if we mean only to make use of that assistance for the purpose of repairing the breach and strengthening the connection between Britain and America; because those powers would be sufferers by the consequences.

Thirdly. While we profess ourselves the subjects of Britain, we must, in the eyes of foreign nations, be considered as rebels. The precedent is somewhat dangerous to *their peace,* for men to be in arms under the name of subjects: we, on the spot, can solve the paradox; but to unite resistance and subjection requires an idea much too refined for common understanding.

Fourthly. Were a manifesto to be published and dispatched to foreign courts, setting forth the miseries we have endured and the peaceful methods which we have ineffectually used for redress; declaring at the same time that, not being able any longer to live happily or safely under the cruel disposition of the British court, we have been driven to the necessity of breaking off all connections with her; at the same time assuring all such courts of our peaceable disposition towards them, and of our desire of entering into trade with them: such a memorial would produce more good effects to this continent, than if a ship were freighted with petitions to Britain.

Under our present denomination of British subjects, we can neither be received nor heard abroad: the custom of all courts is against us, and will be so until by an independence we take rank with other nations.

These proceedings may at first seem strange and difficult, but like all other steps which we have already passed over, will in a little time become familiar and agreeable; and until an Independence is declared, the continent will feel itself like a man who continues putting off some unpleasant business from day to day, yet knows it must be done, hates to set about it, wishes it over, and is continually haunted with the thoughts of its necessity.

COMMON SENSE
by Thomas Paine
1776

I. Facts and Concepts

1. What does this essay try to persuade the colonies to do?

   _____

2. Read the second paragraph and answer the following questions.

   a. Why does Paine say that the "period of debate" about the struggle between England and America is closed?

   _____

   b. Who does Paine blame for ending the debate?

   _____

   c. To what continent is Paine referring when he says, "and the continent has accepted the challenge"?

   _____

3. State the main idea of the third paragraph in your own words.

   _____

   _____

   _____

4. Read the paragraph that begins, "By referring the matter . . . " and answer the following questions.

   a. What event caused the relationship between the colonies and Britain to go "from argument to arms"?

   _____

   b. Before that event, all of the arguments on both sides favored what position?

   _____

   _____

c. Which of the two sides, Britain or the colonies, proposed force in achieving its ends, and which proposed friendship?

_____

_____

5. Read the paragraph that begins, "As much has been . . ." and answer the following questions.

   a. Quote a phrase from this paragraph showing that Paine no longer thought that reconciliation was possible between the colonies and Britain.

   _____

   _____

   b. What four things did Paine say he was going to investigate in the next part of his essay?

   _____

   _____

   _____

   _____

6. Read the paragraph that begins, "I have heard it . . ." and answer the following questions.

   a. What is the first argument about American dependence on Britain that Paine deals with?

   _____

   _____

   _____

   b. Quote the phrase in which Paine refutes this argument.

   _____

   _____

   _____

7. What viewpoint does Paine argue against in the paragraph that begins, "But she has protected . . . "?

_____

_____

8. Read the paragraph that begins, "Alas! we have been . . . " and answer the following questions.

a. What explanation does Paine give for Britain's protection of its American colonies?

_____

_____

b. What does Paine say would be the result of independence in terms of foreign affairs?

_____

_____

9. Read the paragraph that begins, "But Britain is the parent country . . . " and answer the following questions.

a. What viewpoint does Paine argue against in this paragraph?

_____

_____

b. According to Paine, why did most of the people in the colonies flee from Europe?

_____

_____

10. Explain how Paine uses the idea that Britain should be ruled by France in the paragraph that begins, "But, admitting that . . . "

_____

_____

_____

11. Read the paragraph that begins, "Much hath been said . . . " and answer the following questions.

a. What viewpoint does Paine argue against in this paragraph?

_____

_____

b. How does Paine dismiss this argument?

_____

_____

_____

12. According to the paragraph that begins, "Besides, what have we to do . . . ", what will commerce do for America?

_____

_____

_____

13. What does Paine say about American connection with Britain in the paragraph that begins, "I challenge . . . "?

_____

_____

_____

14. In your own words, summarize the main idea of each of the
    paragraphs marked *First* through *Fourthly*.

    _____

    _____

    _____

    _____

    _____

    _____

    _____

    _____

    _____

    _____

II. For Further Understanding

15. Early in the document, Paine speaks of the "commencement
    of hostilities" on "the nineteenth of April." To what event is
    he referring?

    _____

    _____

16. How long after *Common Sense* was published was the
    Declaration of Independence issued?

    _____

17. What European revolution did Paine support after the
    American Revolution? What major work did he write during
    that revolution?

    _____

    _____

18. Look up information on Thomas Paine and write a one-paragraph biography of his life.

_____

_____

_____

_____

_____

_____

_____

_____

_____

DECLARATION OF INDEPENDENCE

1776

The Declaration of Independence expresses the ideas, thoughts, and feelings of a people seeking independence and freedom from oppression. It states the frustrations of the colonists with British rule and announces their intention to form a new nation and government. Its democratic ideas are still used today as examples for people and nations seeking freedom.

When in the Course of human events, it becomes necessary for one people to dissolve the political bands which have connected them with another, and to assume among the Powers of the earth, the separate and equal station to which the Laws of Nature and of Nature's God entitle them, a decent respect to the opinions of mankind requires that they should declare the causes which impel them to the separation.

We hold these truths to be self-evident, that all men are created equal, that they are endowed by their Creator with certain unalienable rights, that among these are Life, Liberty, and the pursuit of Happiness. That to secure these rights, Governments are instituted among Men, deriving their just powers from the consent of the governed, that whenever any Form of Government becomes destructive of these ends, it is the Right of the People to alter or to abolish it, and to institute new Government, laying its foundation on such principles and organizing its powers in such form, as to them shall seem most likely to effect their Safety and Happiness. Prudence, indeed, will dictate that Governments long established should not be changed for light and transient causes; and accordingly all experience hath shown, that mankind are more

disposed to suffer, while evils are sufferable, than to right themselves by abolishing the forms to which they are accustomed. But when a long train of abuses and usurpations, pursuing invariably the same Object evinces a design to reduce them under absolute Despotism, it is their right, it is their duty, to throw off such Government, and to provide new Guards for their future security.—Such has been the patient sufferance of these Colonies; and such is now the necessity which constrains them to alter their former Systems of Government. The history of the present King of Great Britain is a history of repeated injuries and usurpations, all having in direct object the establishment of an absolute Tyranny over these States. To prove this, let Facts be submitted to a candid world.

He has refused his Assent to Laws, the most wholesome and necessary for the public good.

He has forbidden his Governors to pass Laws of immediate and pressing importance, unless suspended in their operation till his Assent should be obtained; and when so suspended, he has utterly neglected to attend to them.

He has refused to pass other Laws for the accommodation of large districts of people, unless those people would relinquish the right of Representation in the Legislature, a right inestimable to them and formidable to tyrants only.

He has called together legislative bodies at places unusual, uncomfortable, and distant from the depository of their Public Records, for the sole purpose of fatiguing them into compliance with his measures.

He has dissolved Representative Houses repeatedly, for

opposing with manly firmness his invasions on the rights of the people.

He has refused for a long time, after such dissolutions, to cause others to be elected; whereby the Legislative Powers, incapable of Annihilation, have returned to the People at large for their exercise; the State remaining in the meantime exposed to all the dangers of invasion from without, and convulsions within.

He has endeavoured to prevent the population of these States; for that purpose obstructing the Laws of Naturalization of Foreigners; refusing to pass others to encourage their migration hither, and raising the conditions of new Appropriations of Lands.

He has obstructed the Administration of Justice, by refusing his Assent to Laws for establishing Judiciary Powers.

He has made Judges dependent on his Will alone, for the tenure of their offices, and the amount and payment of their salaries.

He has erected a multitude of New Offices, and sent hither swarms of Officers to harass our People, and eat out their substance.

He has kept among us in times of peace, Standing Armies without the Consent of our legislatures.

He has affected to render the Military independent of and superior to the Civil Power.

He has combined with others to subject us to a jurisdiction foreign to our constitution, and unacknowledged by our laws; giving his Assent to their acts of pretended legislation:

For quartering large bodies of armed troops among us:

For protecting them, by a mock Trial, from Punishment for any Murders which they should commit on the Inhabitants of these States:

For cutting off our Trade with all parts of the world:

For imposing taxes on us without our Consent:

For depriving us in many cases of the benefits of Trial by Jury:

For transporting us beyond Seas to be tried for pretended offences:

For abolishing the free System of English Laws in a neighbouring Province, establishing therein an Arbitrary government, and enlarging its Boundaries so as to render it at once an example and fit instrument for introducing the same absolute rule into these Colonies:

For taking away our Charters, abolishing our most valuable Laws, and altering fundamentally the Forms of our Governments:

For suspending our own Legislatures, and declaring themselves invested with Power to legislate for us in all cases whatsoever.

He has abdicated Government here, by declaring us out of his Protection, and waging War against us.

He has plundered our seas, ravaged our Coasts, burnt our towns, and destroyed the lives of our people.

He is at this time transporting large armies of foreign mercenaries to compleat the works of death, desolation and tyranny, already begun with circumstances of Cruelty and perfidy scarcely paralleled in the most barbarous ages, and totally unworthy the Head of a civilized nation.

He has constrained our fellow Citizens taken Captive on the high Seas to bear Arms against their Country, to become the executioners of their friends and Brethren, or to fall themselves by their Hands.

He has excited domestic insurrections amongst us, and has endeavoured to bring on the inhabitants of our frontiers the merciless Indian Savages, whose known rule of warfare is an undistinguished destruction of all ages, sexes and conditions.

In every stage of these Oppressions We have Petitioned for Redress, in the most humble terms: Our repeated Petitions have been answered only by repeated injury. A Prince, whose character is thus marked by every act which may define a Tyrant, is unfit to be the ruler of a free People.

Nor have We been wanting in attention to our British brethren. We have warned them from time to time of attempts by their legislature to extend an unwarrantable jurisdiction over us. We have reminded them of the circumstances of our emigration and settlement here. We have appealed to their native justice and magnanimity, and we have conjured them by the ties of our common kindred to disavow these usurpations, which would inevitably interrupt our connections and correspondence. They too have been deaf to the voice of justice and of consanguinity. We must, therefore, acquiesce in the necessity which denounces our Separation, and hold them, as we hold the rest of mankind, Enemies in War, in Peace Friends.

We, therefore, the Representatives of the United States of America, in General Congress, Assembled, appealing to the Supreme Judge of the world for the rectitude of our intentions, do, in the Name and by Authority of the good People of these Colonies, solemnly publish and declare, That these united Colonies are, and of right ought to be Free and Independent states; that they are absolved from all Allegiance to the British Crown, and that all political connection between them and the State of Great Britain is and ought to be totally dissolved; and that as Free and Independent States, they have full Power to levy War, conclude Peace, contract Alliances, establish Commerce, and to do all other Acts and Things which Independent States may of right do. And for the support of this Declaration, with a firm reliance on the Protection of Divine Providence, we mutually pledge to each other our Lives, our Fortunes and our sacred Honor.

DECLARATION OF INDEPENDENCE

1776

I. Facts and Concepts

A. Introductory Paragraphs

1. Quote the phrase in the first paragraph that indicates that the colonies are going to declare their independence.

_____

_____

_____

2. What reason do the authors give in the first paragraph for saying that they must explain why they are declaring independence?

_____

_____

3. Look up the word "unalienable" in a dictionary and write down its definition. What three unalienable rights does the document list?

_____

_____

_____

4. According to this document, what is the purpose for which governments are instituted?

_____

_____

5. From what source do governments get their power?

_____

_____

6. Under what circumstances does the document say a people have a right to overthrow their government?

_____

_____

7. What two-word phrase does the author of the Declaration use to describe the British government over the colonies?

_____

B. Grievances

8. Quote from four grievances detailing abuses by England against the legislative bodies of the colonies.

_____

_____

_____

_____

_____

_____

_____

9. Quote from three grievances describing how England has interfered with the legal system in the colonies.

_____

_____

_____

_____

_____

10. What three groups of people had the British enlisted to fight against the colonists, as stated in three of the grievances?

_____

_____

_____

C. Concluding Paragraphs

11. According to the document, what had the colonists done to try to persuade the British to change their policies?

_____

_____

12. Quote the phrase from the last paragraph in which the colonists officially declare their independence.

_____

_____

_____

_____

13. What powers do the colonies now claim to have as a result of declaring their independence?

_____

_____

II. For Further Understanding

14. Who is the "he" mentioned in the grievances? (Give both his name and his title.)

_____

15. Who wrote the Declaration of Independence?

_____

16. One British action that led many colonists to support the independence movement was the passage of the Intolerable Acts. Look up information on the Intolerable Acts, and find four grievances from the Declaration of Independence that refer to parts of them. For each grievance, tell what action was taken by the British in the Intolerable Acts and then quote the grievance that complains about the action. Here is an example, from an act that was *not* part of the Intolerable Acts:

Action: Armies were brought in to protect the colonists from the Indians and to enforce the Proclamation of 1763. *Grievance:* "He has kept among us in times of peace, standing armies, without the consent of our legislatures."

_____

_____

_____

_____

_____

_____

_____

_____

_____

17. Which two signers of the Declaration of Independence later became presidents of the U.S.?

_____

18. What body governed the colonies from 1776 to 1781?

_____

19. The American Revolution inspired the leaders of a later revolution in Europe. In what country did this revolution take place, and when did it break out?

_____

THE CRISIS
by Thomas Paine

1776

The Crisis was a series of pamphlets written by Thomas Paine during the American Revolution. Paine's purpose in writing the pamphlets was to renew the enthusiasm that had sparked the revolution. He inspired many Americans to continue the fight against Great Britain.

These are the times that try men's souls. The summer soldier and the sunshine patriot will, in this crisis, shrink from the service of his country; but he that stands it *now,* deserves the love and thanks of man and woman. Tyranny, like hell, is not easily conquered; yet we have this consolation with us, that the harder the conflict, the more glorious the triumph. What we obtain too cheap, we esteem too lightly: it is dearness only that gives everything its value. Heaven knows how to put a proper price upon its goods; and it would be strange indeed if so celestial an article as FREEDOM should not be highly rated. Britain, with an army to enforce her tyranny, has declared that she has a right (*not only to* TAX) but "to BIND *us in* ALL CASES WHATSOEVER"; and if being *bound in that manner* is not slavery, then is there such a thing as slavery upon earth. Even the expression is impious; for so unlimited a power can belong only to God.

Whether the independence of the continent was declared too soon, or delayed too long, I will not now enter into as an argument; my own simple opinion is, that had it been eight months earlier it would have been much better. We did not make a proper use of last winter; neither could we, while we were in a dependent state. However, the fault, if it were one, was all our own; we have none to blame but ourselves. But no great deal is lost yet. All that Howe has been doing for this month past is rather a ravage than a conquest, which the spirit of the Jerseys a year ago would have quickly repulsed, and which time and a little resolution will soon recover.

I have as little superstition in me as any man living; but my secret opinion has ever been, and still is, that God Almighty will not give up a people to military destruction, or leave them unsupportedly to perish, who have so earnestly and so repeatedly sought to avoid the calamities of war, by every decent method which wisdom could invent. Neither have I so much of the infidel in me as to suppose that he has relinquished the government of the world, and given us up to the care of devils; and as I do not, I cannot see on what grounds the king of Britain can look up to heaven for help against us: a common murderer, a highwayman, or a housebreaker, has as good a pretense as he.

As I was with the troops at Fort Lee, and marched with them to the edge of Pennsylvania, I am well acquainted with many circumstances which those who live at a distance know but little or nothing of. Our situation there was exceedingly cramped, the place being a narrow neck of land between the North River and the Hackensack. Our force was inconsiderable, being not one-fourth so great as Howe could bring against us. We had no army at hand to have relieved the garrison, had we shut ourselves up and stood on our defense. Our ammunition, light artillery, and the best part of our stores, had been removed, on the apprehension that Howe would endeavor to penetrate the Jerseys, in which case Fort Lee could be of no use to us; for it must occur to every thinking man, whether in the army or not, that these kind of field forts are only for temporary purposes, and last in use no longer than the enemy directs his force against the particular object which such forts are raised to defend. Such was our situation and condition at Fort Lee on the morning of the 20th of November, when an officer arrived with information that the enemy with 200 boats had landed about seven miles above. Major General Green, who commanded the garrison, immediately ordered them under arms, and sent express to General Washington at the town of Hackensack, distant by the way of the ferry, six miles. Our first object was to secure the bridge over the Hackensack, which laid up the river between the enemy and us, about six miles from us, three from them. General Washington arrived in about three-quarters of an hour, and marched at the head of the troops towards the bridge, which place I expected we should have a brush for; however, they did not choose to dispute it with us, and the greatest part of our troops went over the bridge, the rest over the ferry, except some which passed at a mill on a small creek between the bridge and the ferry, and made their way through some marshy grounds up to the town of Hackensack, and there passed the river. We brought off as much baggage as the wagons could contain, the rest was lost. The simple object was to bring off the garrison and march them on till they could be strengthened by the Jersey or Pennsylvania militia,

so as to be enabled to make a stand. We staid four days at Newark, collected our outposts with some of the Jersey militia, and marched out twice to meet the enemy on being informed that they were advancing, though our numbers were greatly inferior to theirs. Howe, in my little opinion, committed a great error in generalship in not throwing a body of forces off from Staten Island through Amboy, by which means he might have seized all our stores at Brunswick and intercepted our march into Pennsylvania; but if we believe the power of hell to be limited, we must likewise believe that their agents are under some providential control.

I shall not now attempt to give all the particulars of our retreat to the Delaware; suffice it for the present to say that both officers and men, though greatly harassed and fatigued, frequently without rest, covering, or provision—the inevitable consequences of a long retreat—bore it with a manly and martial spirit. All their wishes centered in one; which was, that the country would turn out and help them to drive the enemy back. Voltaire has remarked that King William never appeared to full advantage but in difficulties and in action; the same remark may be made on General Washington, for the character fits him. There is a natural firmness in some minds which cannot be unlocked by trifles, but which, when unlocked, discovers a cabinet of fortitude; and I reckon it among those kinds of public blessings, which we do not immediately see, that God hath blessed him with uninterrupted health, and given him a mind that can even flourish upon care.

I turn with the warm ardor of

a friend to those who have nobly stood, and are yet determined to stand the matter out: I call not upon a few, but upon all: not on *this* State or *that* State, but on *every* State: up and help us; lay your shoulders to the wheel; better have too much force than too little, when so great an object is at stake. Let it be told to the future world, that in the depth of winter, when nothing but hope and virtue could survive, that the city and the country, alarmed at one common danger, came forth to meet and to repulse it. Say not that thousands are gone—turn out your tens of thousands; throw not the burden of the day upon Providence, but *"show your faith by your works,"* that God may bless you. It matters not where you live, or what rank of life you hold, the evil or the blessing will reach you all. The far and the near, the home counties and the back, the rich and the poor, will suffer or rejoice alike. The heart that feels not now is dead; the blood of his children will curse his cowardice who shrinks back at a time when a little might have saved the whole and made *them* happy. I love the man that can smile in trouble, that can gather strength from distress and grow brave by reflection. It is the business of little minds to shrink; but he whose heart is firm, and whose conscience approves his conduct, will pursue his principles unto death. My own line of reasoning is to myself as straight and clear as a ray of light. Not all the treasures of the world, so far as I believe, could have induced me to support an offensive war, for I think it murder; but if a thief breaks into my house, burns and destroys my property, and kills or threatens to kill me or those that are in it, and to *"bind me in all cases*

whatsoever" to his absolute will, am I to suffer it? What signifies it to me whether he who does it is a king or a common man; my countryman or not my countryman; whether it be done by an individual villain, or an army of them? If we reason to the root of things we shall find no difference; neither can any just cause be assigned why we should punish in the one case and pardon in the other. Let them call me rebel and welcome—I feel no concern from it; but I should suffer the misery of devils, were I to make a whore of my soul by swearing allegiance to one whose character is that of a scottish, stupid, stubborn, worthless, brutish man. I conceive likewise a horrid idea in receiving mercy from a being, who at the last day shall be shrieking to the rocks and mountains to cover him, and fleeing with terror from the orphan, the widow, and the slain of America.

I thank God that I fear not. I see no real cause for fear. I know our situation well, and can see the way out of it. While our army was collected, Howe dared not risk a battle; and it is no credit to him that he decamped from the White Plains, and waited a mean opportunity to ravage the defenseless Jerseys; but it is great credit to us, that with a handful of men, we sustained an orderly retreat for near a hundred miles, brought off our ammunition, all our fieldpieces, the greatest part of our stores, and had four rivers to pass. None can say that our retreat was precipitate; for we were near three weeks in performing it, that the country might have time to come in.

Twice we marched back to meet the enemy, and remained out till dark. The sign of fear was not seen in our camp, and had not

38

some of the cowardly and disaffected inhabitants spread false alarms through the country, the Jerseys had never been ravaged. Once more we are again collected and collecting, our new army at both ends of the continent is recruiting fast, and we shall be able to open the next campaign with sixty thousand men, well-armed and clothed. This is our situation, and who will may know it. By perseverance and fortitude we have the prospect of a glorious issue; by cowardice and submission, the sad choice of a variety of evils: a ravaged country—a depopulated city—habitations without safety, and slavery without hope—our homes turned into barracks and bawdy-houses for Hessians—and a future race to provide for, whose fathers we shall doubt of. Look on this picture and weep over it! and if there yet remains one thoughtless wretch who believes it not, let him suffer it unlamented.

THE CRISIS
by Thomas Paine
1776

I. Facts and Concepts

1. Read the first paragraph of this document and answer the following questions.

   a. What does Paine mean by the "summer soldier" and the "sunshine patriot"?

   _____

   _____

   b. Why does freedom have such a high price, according to Paine?

   _____

   c. How does Paine try to provoke the anger of the colonists at the end of this paragraph?

   _____

   _____

   _____

2. What opinion about the Declaration of Independence does Paine reveal in the second paragraph? Give a quotation from the paragraph to support your answer.

   _____

   _____

   _____

3. Read the paragraph that begins, "I have as little superstition . . . " and answer the following questions.

   a. Why does Paine believe that God is on the side of the colonists?

   _____

   _____

b. Why does Paine believe that God would not support the king of England?

_____

_____

4. Read the paragraph that begins, "As I was with . . ." and answer the following questions.

a. In the battle described here, what was the size of the colonial army in comparison to the British?

_____

b. What general commanded the British troops at this battle?

_____

c. At what fort were the American troops garrisoned? Who commanded that fort?

_____

_____

d. Who commanded all of the American troops?

_____

e. What two things were the American troops trying to accomplish?

_____

_____

5. In the paragraph that begins, "I shall not now attempt . . ." how does Paine describe the condition of the soldiers who marched with Washington during the campaign in New Jersey?

_____

_____

6. Read the paragraph that begins, "I turn with . . ." and answer the following questions.

a. What does Paine urge the colonies to do in this paragraph?

_____

b. What is Paine's "own line of reasoning" about the war?

_____

_____

c. Who was the "scottish, stupid, stubborn, worthless, brutish man" described in this paragraph?

_____

7. Read the paragraph that begins, "I thank God . . ." and answer the following questions.

a. What phrase does Paine use to reassure the colonists about the war?

_____

_____

b. For what does Paine praise the American army?

_____

_____

_____

8. Read the paragraph that begins, "Twice we marched back . . ." and answer the following questions.

a. According to Paine, what will be the condition of the army in the next campaign?

_____

_____

b. What "variety of evils" does Paine say would result if the colonists chose "cowardice and submission" towards the British?

_____

_____

_____

II. For Further Understanding

9. Give a brief account of the events at the beginning of the revolutionary war. Why did Paine want to renew the initial enthusiasm of the colonists?

_____

_____

_____

_____

_____

_____

10. What was the site of Washington's first victory, which occurred on December 25, 1776, shortly after *The Crisis* was published?

_____

11. To what law passed by the British Parliament was Paine referring when he said that Britain gave itself the power "to bind us in all cases whatsoever?"

_____

12. What was the capital of the colonies during the revolutionary war? How did the British advance described in this document affect the capital?

_____

_____

_____

ARTICLES OF CONFEDERATION

1781

In June 1776 the Continental Congress appointed a committee to draw up a plan of government for the independent colonies. This committee wrote the Articles of Confederation, which were sent to Congress in July 1776. After a long process of debate and revision, the Articles were approved on November 15, 1777, and sent to the states for ratification. They were ratified in 1781. Although the Confederation proved to be an unwieldy government, many ideas contained in the Articles later appeared in the Constitution.

TO ALL TO WHOM these Presents shall come, we the undersigned Delegates of the States affixed to our Names send greeting. Whereas the Delegates of the United States of America in Congress assembled did on the fifteenth day of November in the Year of our Lord One Thousand Seven Hundred and Seventy seven, and in the Second Year of the Independence of America agree to certain articles of Confederation and perpetual Union between the States of Newhampshire, Massachusetts-bay, Rhodeisland and Providence Plantations, Connecticut, New York, New Jersey, Pennsylvania, Delaware, Maryland, Virginia, North-Carolina, South-Carolina and Georgia in the Words following, viz. "Articles of Confederation and perpetual Union between the states of Newhampshire, Massachusetts-bay, Rhodeisland and Providence Plantations, Connecticut, New-York, New-Jersey, Pennsylvania, Delaware, Maryland, Virginia, North-Carolina, South-Carolina and Georgia.

Article I. The Stile of this confederacy shall be "The United States of America."

Article II. Each state retains its sovereignty, freedom and independence, and every Power, Jurisdiction and right, which is not by this confederation expressly delegated to the United States, in Congress assembled.

Article III. The said states hereby severally enter into a firm league of friendship with each other, for their common defence, the security of their Liberties, and their mutual and general welfare, binding themselves to assist each other, against all force offered to, or attacks made upon them, or any of them, on account of religion, sovereignty, trade, or any other pretence whatever.

Article IV. The better to secure and perpetuate mutual friendship and intercourse among the people of the different states in this union, the free inhabitants of each of these states, paupers, vagabonds and fugitives from Justice excepted, shall be entitled to all privileges and immunities of free citizens in the several states; and the people of each state shall have free ingress and regress to and from any other state, and shall enjoy therein all the privileges of trade and commerce, subject to the same duties, impositions and restrictions as the inhabitants thereof respectively, provided that such restriction shall not extend so far as to prevent the removal of property imported into any state, to any other state of which the Owner is an inhabitant; provided also that no imposition, duties or restrictions shall be laid by any state, on the property of the united states, or either of them.

If any Person guilty of, or charged with treason, felony, or other high misdemeanor in any state, shall flee from Justice, and be found in any of the united states, he shall upon demand of the Governor or executive power, of the state from which he fled, be delivered up and removed to the state having jurisdiction of his offence.

Full faith and credit shall be given in each of these states to the records, acts and judicial proceedings of the courts and magistrates of every other state.

Article V. For the more convenient management of the general interests of the united states, delegates shall be annually appointed in such manner as the legislature of each state shall direct, to meet in Congress on the first Monday in November, in every year, with a power reserved to each state, to recal its delegates, or any of them, at any time within the year, and to send others in their stead, for the remainder of the Year.

No state shall be represented in Congress by less than two, nor by more than seven Members; and no person shall be capable of being a delegate for more than three years in any term of six years; nor shall any person, being a delegate, be capable of holding any office under the united states, for which he, or another for his benefit receives any salary, fees or emolument of any kind.

Each state shall maintain its own delegates in a meeting of the states, and while they act as members of the committee of the states.

In determining questions in the united states, in Congress assembled, each state shall have one vote.

Freedom of speech and debate in Congress shall not be impeached or questioned in any Court, or place out of Congress, and the members of congress shall be protected in their persons from arrests and imprisonments, during the time of their going to and from, and attendance on congress, except for treason, felony, or breach of the peace.

Article VI. No state without the Consent of the united states in congress assembled, shall send any embassy to, or receive any embassy from, or enter into any conference, agreement, or alliance or treaty with any King, prince or state; nor shall any person holding any office of profit or trust under the united states, or any of them, accept of any present, emolument, office or title of any kind whatever from any king, prince or foreign state; nor shall the united states in congress assembled, or any of them, grant any title of nobility.

No two or more states shall enter into any treaty, confederation or alliance whatever between them, without the consent of the united states in congress assembled, specifying accurately the purposes for which the same is to be entered into, and how long it shall continue.

No state shall lay any imposts or duties, which may interfere with any stipulations in treaties, entered into by the united states in congress assembled, with any king, prince or state, in pursuance of any treaties already proposed by congress, to the courts of France and Spain.

No vessels of war shall be kept up in time of peace by any state, except such number only, as shall be deemed necessary by the united states in congress assembled, for the defence of such state, or its trade; nor shall any body of forces be kept up by any state, in time of peace, except such number only, as in the judgment of the united states, in congress assembled, shall be deemed requisite to garrison the forts necessary for the defence of such state; but every state shall always keep up a well regulated and disciplined militia, sufficiently armed and accoutred, and shall provide and constantly have ready for use, in public stores, a due number of field pieces and tents, and a proper quantity of arms, ammunition and camp equipage.

No state shall engage in any war without the consent of the united states in congress assembled, unless such state be actually invaded by enemies, or shall have received certain advice of a resolution being formed by some nation of Indians to invade such state, and the danger is so imminent as not to admit of a delay, till the united states in congress assembled can be consulted: nor shall any state grant commissions to any ships or vessels of war, nor letters of marque or reprisal, except it be after a declaration of war by the united states in congress assembld, and then only against the kingdom or state and the subjects thereof, against which war has been so declared, and under such regulations as shall be established by the united states in congress assembled, unless such state be infested by pirates, in which case vessels of war may be fitted out for that occasion, and kept so long as the danger shall continue, or until the united states in congress assembled shall determine otherwise.

Article VII. When land-forces are raised by any state for the common defence, all officers of or under the rank of colonel, shall be appointed by the legislature of each state respectively by whom such forces shall be raised, or in such manner as such state shall direct, and all vacancies shall be filled up by the state which first made the appointment.

Article VIII. All charges of war, and all other expences that shall be incurred for the common defence or general welfare, and allowed by the united states in congress assembled, shall be defrayed out of a common treasury, which shall be supplied by the several states, in proportion to the value of all land within each state, granted to or surveyed for any Person, as such land and the buildings and improvements thereon shall be estimated according to such mode as the united states in congress assembled, shall from time to time direct and appoint. The taxes for paying that proportion shall be laid and levied by the authority and direction of the legislatures of the several states within the time agreed upon by the united states in congress assembled.

Article IX. The united states in congress assembled, shall have the sole and exclusive right and power of determining on peace and war, except in the cases mentioned in the sixth article—of sending and receiving ambassadors— entering into treaties and alliances, provided that no treaty of commerce shall be made whereby the legislative power of the respective states shall be restrained from imposing such imposts and duties on foreigners, as their own people are subjected to, or from prohibiting the exportation or importation of any species of goods or commodities whatsoever—of establishing rules for deciding in all cases, what captures on land or water shall be legal, and in what manner prizes taken by land or naval forces in the service of the united states shall be divided or appropriated.— of granting letters of marque and reprisal in times of peace— appointing courts for the trial of piracies and felonies committed on the high seas and establishing courts for receiving and determining finally appeals in all cases of captures, provided that no member of congress shall be appointed a judge of any of the said courts.

The united states in congress assembled shall also be the last resort on appeal in all disputes and differences now subsisting or that hereafter may arise between two or more states concerning boundary, jurisdiction or any other cause whatever; which authority shall always be exercised in the manner following. Whenever the legislative or executive authority or lawful agent of any state in controversy with another shall present a petition to congress, stating the matter in question and praying for a hearing, notice thereof shall be given by order of congress to the legislative or executive authority of the other state in controversy, and a day assigned for the appearance of the parties by their lawful agents, who shall then be directed to appoint by joint consent, commissioners or judges to constitute a court for hearing and determining the matter in question: but if they cannot agree, congress shall name three persons out of each of the united states, and from the list of such persons each party shall alternately strike out one, the petitioners beginning, until the number shall be reduced to thirteen; and from that number not less than seven, nor more than nine names as congress shall direct, shall in the presence of congress be drawn out by lot, and the persons whose names shall be so drawn or any five of them, shall be commissioners or judges, to hear and finally determine the controversy, so always as a major part of the

judges who shall hear the cause shall agree in the determination: and if either party shall neglect to attend at the day appointed, without shewing reasons, which congress shall judge sufficient, or being present shall refuse to strike, the congress shall proceed to nominate three persons out of each state, and the secretary of congress shall strike in behalf of such party absent or refusing; and the judgment and sentence of the court to be appointed, in the manner before prescribed, shall be final and conclusive; and if any of the parties shall refuse to submit to the authority of such court, or to appear to defend their claim or cause, the court shall nevertheless proceed to pronounce sentence, or judgment, which shall in like manner be final and decisive, the judgment or sentence and other proceedings being in either case transmitted to congress, and lodged among the acts of congress for the security of the parties concerned; provided that every commissioner, before he sits in judgment, shall take an oath to be administered by one of the judges of the supreme or superior court of the state, where the cause shall be tried, "well and truly to hear and determine the matter in question, according to the best of his judgment, without favour, affection or hope of reward:" provided also that no state shall be deprived of territory for the benefit of the united states.

All controversies concerning the private right of soil claimed under different grants of two or more states, whose jurisdictions as they may respect such lands, and the states which passed such grants are adjusted, the said grants or either of them being at the same time claimed to have originated antecedent to such

48

settlement of jurisdiction, shall on the petition of either party to the congress of the united states, be finally determined as near as may be in the same manner as is before prescribed for deciding disputes respecting territorial jurisdiction between different states.

The united states in congress assembled shall also have the sole and exclusive right and power of regulating the alloy and value of coin struck by their own authority, or by that of the respective states—fixing the standard of weights and measures throughout the united states.—regulating the trade and managing all affairs with the Indians, not members of any of the states, provided that the legislative right of any state within its own limits be not infringed or violated—establishing and regulating post-offices from one state to another, throughout all the united states, and exacting such postage on the papers passing thro' the same as may be requisite to defray the expences of the said office—appointing all officers of the land forces, in the service of the united states, excepting regimental officers—appointing all the officers of the naval forces, and commissioning all officers whatever in the service of the united states—making rules for the government and regulation of the said land and naval forces, and directing their operations.

The united states in congress assembled shall have authority to appoint a committee, to sit in the recess of congress, to be denominated "A Committee of the States," and to consist of one delegate from each state; and to appoint such other committees and civil officers as may be necessary for managing the general affairs of the united states under their direction—to appoint one of their number to preside, provided that no person be allowed to serve in the office of president more than one year in any term of three years; to ascertain the necessary sums of Money to be raised for the service of the united states, and to appropriate and apply the same for defraying the public expences—to borrow money, or emit bills on the credit of the united states, transmitting every half year to the respective states an account of the sums of money so borrowed or emitted,—to build and equip a navy—to agree upon the number of land forces, and to make requisitions from each state for its quota, in proportion to the number of white inhabitants in such state; which requisition shall be binding, and thereupon the legislature of each state shall appoint the regimental officers, raise the men and cloath, arm and equip them in a soldier like manner, at the expence of the united states, and the officers and men so cloathed, armed and equipped shall march to the place appointed, and within the time agreed on by the united states in congress assembled: But if the united states in congress assembled shall, on consideration of circumstances judge proper that any state should not raise men, or should raise a smaller number than its quota, and that any other state should raise a greater number of men than the quota thereof, such extra number shall be raised, officered, cloathed, armed and equipped in the same manner as the quota of such state, unless the legislature of such state shall judge that such extra number cannot be safely spared out of the same, in which case they shall raise officer, cloath, arm and equip as many of such extra number as they judge can be safely spared. And the officers and men so cloathed, armed and equipped, shall march to the place appointed, and within the time agreed on by the united states in congress assembled.

The united states in congress assembled shall never engage in a war, nor grant letters of marque and reprisal in time of peace, nor enter into any treaties or alliances, nor coin money, nor regulate the value thereof, nor ascertain the sums and expences necessary for the defence and welfare of the united states, or any of them, nor emit bills, nor borrow money on the credit of the united states, nor appropriate money, nor agree upon the number of vessels of war, to be built or purchased, or the number of land or sea forces to be raised, nor appoint a commander in chief of the army or navy, unless nine states assent to the same: nor shall a question on any other point, except for adjourning from day to day be determined, unless by the votes of a majority of the united states in congress assembled.

The congress of the united states shall have power to adjourn to any time within the year, and to any place within the united states, so that no period of adjournment be for a longer duration than the space of six Months, and shall publish the Journal of their proceedings monthly, except such parts thereof relating to treaties, alliances or military operations as in their judgment require secresy; and the yeas and nays of the delegates of each state on any question shall be entered on the Journal, when it is desired by any delegate; and the delegates of a state, or any of them, at his or their request shall be furnished with a transcript of the said Journal, except such parts as are

above excepted, to lay before the legislatures of the several states.

Article X. The committee of the states, or any nine of them, shall be authorised to execute, in the recess of congress, such of the powers of congress as the united states in congress assembled, by the consent of nine states, shall from time to time think expedient to vest them with; provided that no power be delegated to the said committee, for the exercise of which, by the articles of confederation, the voice of nine states in the congress of the united states assembled is requisite.

Article XI. Canada acceding to this confederation, and joining in the measures of the united states, shall be admitted into, and entitled to all the advantages of this union: but no other colony shall be admitted into the same, unless such admission be agreed to by nine states.

Article XII. All bills of credit emitted, monies borrowed and debts contracted by, or under the authority of congress, before the assembling of the united states, in pursuance of the present confederation, shall be deemed and considered as a charge against the united states, for payment and satisfaction whereof the said united states, and the public faith are hereby solemnly pledged.

Article XIII. Every state shall abide by the determinations of the united states in congress assembled, on all questions which by this confederation are submitted to them. And the Articles of this confederation shall be inviolably observed by every state, and the union shall be perpetual; nor shall any alteration at any time hereafter be made in any of them; unless such alteration be agreed to in a congress of the united states, and be afterwards confirmed by the legislatures of every state.

AND WHEREAS it hath pleased the Great Governor of the World to incline the hearts of the legislatures we respectively represent in congress, to approve of, and to authorize us to ratify the said articles of confederation and perpetual union. KNOW YE that we the under-signed delegates, by virtue of the power and authority to us given for that purpose, do by these presents, in the name and in behalf of our respective constituents, fully and entirely ratify and confirm each and every of the said articles of confederation and perpetual union, and all and singular the matters and things therein contained: And we do further solemnly plight and engage the faith of our respective constituents, that they shall abide by the determinations of the united states in congress assembled, on all questions, which by the said confederation are submitted to them. And that the articles thereof shall be inviolably observed by the states we respectively represent, and that the union shall be perpetual. In Witness whereof we have hereunto set our hands in Congress. Done at Philadelphia in the state of Pennsylvania the ninth Day of July in the Year of our Lord one Thousand seven Hundred and Seventy-eight, and in the third year of the independence of America.

ARTICLES OF CONFEDERATION
1781

I. Facts and Concepts

1. What was the name of the confederacy formed under this document?

    _____

2. Explain in your own words the guarantee of Article II.

    _____

    _____

    _____

3. According to Article III, what were the three purposes for which the states organized into a confederation?

    _____

    _____

    _____

4. Read Article IV and answer the following questions.

    a. The "free inhabitants of each of these states" were entitled to what consideration by all of the states?

    _____

    _____

    b. Look up the words "ingress" and "regress" in a dictionary and write down their meanings.

    _____

    _____

    c. What is the right of "free ingress and regress" described here?

    _____

d. Look up the word "extradition" and write down its meaning. Which of the paragraphs in this article provided for extradition among the states? Give a quotation from the paragraph to support your answer.

_____

_____

_____

_____

_____

e. The third paragraph of this article says that all states must respect what actions of the other states?

_____

_____

5. Read Article V and answer the following questions.

a. Who or what body determined the method by which delegates were selected for Congress?

_____

b. Why would the states want to have the power to recall their delegates and send new ones to Congress?

_____

_____

_____

c. How many delegates could each state send to Congress?

_____

d. How many years could any one person serve as a delegate to Congress?

_____

e. How many votes did each state have in Congress?

_____

f. What two guarantees for members of Congress are
included in the last paragraph of this article?

_____

_____

6. Read Article VI and answer the following questions.

a. Could North Carolina send an ambassador to Holland to
ask for its help in the revolutionary war? Give a quotation from this article to support your answer.

_____

_____

_____

b. If the U.S. made a treaty with Spain saying that Spain
could export goods to the U.S. without paying a tax,
could Massachusetts and Pennsylvania put a tax on
those goods as they entered their states? Give a quotation from this article to support your answer.

_____

_____

_____

_____

c. Could George Washington have been made a duke by
Congress as a reward for his services during the revolutionary war? Give a quotation from this article to support your answer.

_____

_____

d. Could Maryland and Virginia have formed an alliance without the consent of Congress? Give a quotation from this article to support your answer.

_____

_____

_____

_____

e. States were not allowed to keep standing armies during peacetime, but what group could they use to defend themselves? Give a quotation from this article to support your answer.

_____

_____

_____

f. Could Georgia go to war to defend itself against a Spanish invasion without consulting Congress? Give a quotation from this article to support your answer.

_____

_____

_____

7. Read Article VIII and answer the following questions.

a. What types of debts would the confederation pay for?

_____

_____

b. On what basis was the amount of tax each state had to pay to the confederation to be figured?

_____

c. Who had the power to lay taxes, the confederation or the states? Give a quotation from this article to support your answer.

_____

_____

_____

8. Read Article IX and answer the following questions.

a. List in your own words the powers granted to the confederation in the first paragraph of this article.

_____

_____

_____

_____

_____

b. Congress was "the last resort on appeal" for what disputes mentioned in the second paragraph of this article?

_____

_____

c. From whom did the commissioners or judges of the confederation have to take an oath before they could decide a case?

_____

_____

d. What powers are granted to Congress in the fourth paragraph of this article?

_____

_____

_____

_____

_____

_____

e. What powers are granted to Congress in the fifth paragraph of this article?

_____

_____

_____

_____

f. According to the sixth paragraph of this article, how many states had to approve the actions of Congress before they could take effect?

_____

_____

9. Suppose that the people of Florida wanted their colony to join the United States under the Articles of Confederation. According to Article XI, what would have to happen before Florida could be admitted as a state?

_____

_____

10. What did the confederation pledge to do in Article XII?

_____

_____

11. Read Article XIII and answer the following questions.

    a. State in your own words the main idea of the first
       sentence of this article.

_____

_____

_____

    b. What does this article say about amending the Articles
       of Confederation?

_____

_____

12. According to the last paragraph, what did the signers of
the Articles of Confederation guarantee by their
signatures?

_____

_____

_____

II. For Further Understanding

13. The Articles of Confederation provided for only one branch
of government, while the Constitution provides for three.
Which two branches of our present government were left
out of the Articles of Confederation?

_____

_____

14. Look up more information on the Articles of Confederation
and list two of its major weaknesses.

_____

_____

_____

15. Why did Maryland not ratify the Articles of Confederation until much later than the other states?

_____

_____

_____

_____

16. Between the date when the U.S. declared its independence and the date when the Articles of Confederation went into effect, what body governed the United States?

_____

LAND ORDINANCE OF 1785

1785

Westward migration beyond the thirteen states created problems for the young American government. Yet the government proved itself worthy of handling these problems with the Land Ordinance of 1785, which established a system of surveying, dividing, and selling land.

Be it ordained by the United States in Congress assembled, that the territory ceded by individual States to the United States, which has been purchased of the Indian inhabitants, shall be disposed of in the following manner:

A surveyor from each state shall be appointed by Congress or a Committee of the States, who shall take an oath for the faithful discharge of his duty, before the Geographer of the United States . . .

The Surveyors, as they are respectively qualified, shall proceed to divide the said territory into townships of six miles square, by lines running due north and south, and others crossing these at right angles, as near as may be, unless where the boundaries of the late Indian purchases may render the same impracticable, . . .

The first line, running due north and south as aforesaid, shall begin on the river Ohio, at a point that shall be found to be due north from the western termination of a line, which has been run as the southern boundary of the State of Pennsylvania; and the first line, running east and west, shall begin at the same point, and shall extend throughout the whole territory. Provided, that nothing herein shall be construed, as fixing the western boundary of the State of Pennsylvania. The geographer shall designate the townships, or fractional parts of townships, by numbers progressively from south to north; always beginning each range with No. 1; and the ranges shall be distinguished by their progressive numbers to the westward. The first range, extending from the Ohio to the lake Erie, being marked No. 1. The Geographer shall personally attend to the running of the first east and west line; and shall take the latitude of the extremes of the first north and south line, and of the mouths of the principal rivers.

The lines shall be measured with a chain; shall be plainly marked by chaps on the trees, and exactly described on a plat; whereon shall be noted by the surveyor, at their proper distances, all mines, salt-springs, salt-licks and mill-seats, that shall come to his knowledge, and all water-courses, mountains and other remarkable and permanent things, over and near which such lines shall pass, and also the quality of the lands.

The plat of the townships respectively, shall be marked by subdivisions into lots of one mile square, or 640 acres, in the same direction as the external lines, and numbered from 1 to 36; always beginning the succeeding range of the lots with the number next to that with which the preceding one concluded . . .

And the geographer shall make . . . returns, from time to time, of every seven ranges as they may be surveyed. The Secretary of War shall have recourse thereto, and shall take by lot therefrom, a number of townships . . . as will be equal to one seventh part of the whole of such seven ranges, . . . for the use of the late Continental army . . .

The board of treasury shall transmit a copy of the original plats, previously noting thereon the townships and fractional parts of townships, which shall have fallen to the several states, by the distribution aforesaid, to the commissioners of the loan-office of the several states, who, after giving notice ... shall proceed to sell the townships or fractional parts of townships, at public vendue, in the following manner, viz.: The township or fractional part of a township No. 1, in the first range, shall be sold entire; and No. 2, in the same range, by lots; and thus in alternate order through the whole of the first range ... provided, that none of the lands, within the said territory, be sold under the price of one dollar the acre, to be paid in specie, or loan-office certificates, reduced to specie value, by the scale of depreciation, or certificates of liquidated debts of the United States, including interest, besides the expense of the survey and other charges thereon, which are hereby rated at thirty six dollars the township, ... on failure of which payment, the said lands shall again be offered for sale.

There shall be reserved for the United States out of every township the four lots, being numbered 8,11,26,29, and out of every fractional part of a township, so many lots of the same numbers as shall be found thereon, for future sale. There shall be reserved the lot No. 16, of every township, for the maintenance of public schools within the said township; also one-third part of all gold, silver, lead and copper mines, to be sold, or otherwise disposed of as Congress shall hereafter direct ...

And Whereas Congress ... stipulated grants of land to certain officers and soldiers of the late Continental army ... for complying with such engagements, Be it ordained, That the secretary of war ... determine who are the objects of the above resolutions and engagements ... and cause the townships, or fractional parts of townships, herein before reserved for the use of the late Continental army, to be drawn for in such manner as he shall deem expedient ...

LAND ORDINANCE OF 1785

1785

I. Facts and Concepts

1. According to the first paragraph of the ordinance, what
   two conditions determined the types of land that came
   under its jurisdiction?

   _____

   _____

2. The second paragraph says that "A surveyor from each
   state shall be appointed by Congress or a Committee of the
   States, . . . " Why was it important that all of the states be
   involved in the reorganization of land?

   _____

   _____

   _____

   _____

3. What size were townships created under this document?

   _____

4. According to the fourth paragraph of the document, what
   did the Geographer of the United States have to do to
   make sure that the survey was accurate?

   _____

   _____

   _____

5. Look up the words "chap," "plat," and "specie" in a
   dictionary and write down their definitions as they are used
   in this document.

   _____

   _____

   _____

6. According to the paragraph that begins, "And the geographer..." for what purpose was some of the surveyed land to be reserved?

_____

_____

_____

7. According to the paragraph that begins, "The board of treasury..." what was the minimum price for an acre of land under this ordinance?

_____

8. Read the paragraph that begins, "There shall be reserved..." and answer the following questions.

    a. For what purpose was lot number 16 of each township to be reserved?

    _____

    b. What share of the mining resources of each township was to be reserved for the U.S. government?

    _____

II. For Further Understanding

9. For what territory was the Land Ordinance of 1785 originally designed?

_____

_____

_____

10. How long did the Land Ordinance of 1785 govern the division and sale of western lands?

_____

11. What law replaced the Land Ordinance of 1785?

_____

12. What form of national government was the U.S. under when the Land Ordinance of 1785 was passed?

_____

VIRGINIA STATUTE OF RELIGIOUS LIBERTY

1786

The Virginia Statute of Religious Liberty was introduced in the Virginia Assembly in 1779 and passed in 1786. The statute, a monument to the doctrine of separation of church and state, provided a model for the authors of the Bill of Rights of the U.S. Constitution.

I. WHEREAS Almighty God hath created the mind free; that all attempts to influence it by temporal punishments or burthens, or by civil incapacitations, tend only to beget habits of hypocrisy and meanness, and are a departure from the plan of the Holy author of our religion, who being Lord both of body and mind, yet chose not to propagate it by coercions on either, as was in his Almighty power to do; that the impious presumption of legislators and rulers, civil as well as ecclesiastical, who being themselves but fallible and uninspired men, have assumed dominion over the faith of others, setting up their own opinions and modes of thinking as the only true and infallible, and as such endeavouring to impose them on others, hath established and maintained false religions over the greatest part of the world, and through all time; that to compel a man to furnish contributions of money for the propagation of opinions which he disbelieves, is sinful and tyrannical; that even the forcing him to support this or that teacher of his own religious persuasion, is depriving him of the comfortable liberty of giving his contributions to the particular pastor whose morals he would make his pattern, and whose powers he feels most persuasive to righteousness, and is withdrawing from the ministry those temporary rewards, which proceeding from an approbation of their personal conduct, are an additional incitement to earnest and unremitting labours for the instruction of mankind; that our civil rights have no dependence on our religious opinions, any more than our opinions in physics or geometry; that therefore the proscribing any citizen as unworthy the public confidence by laying upon him an incapacity of being called to offices of trust and emolument, unless he profess or renounce this or that religious opinion, is depriving him injuriously of those privileges and advantages to which in common with his fellow-citizens he has a natural right, that it tends only to corrupt the principles of that religion it is meant to encourage, by bribing with a monopoly of worldly honours and emoluments, those who will externally profess and conform to it; that though indeed these are criminal who do not withstand such temptation, yet neither are those innocent who lay the bait in their way; that to suffer the civil magistrate to intrude his powers into the field of opinion, and to restrain the profession or propagation of principles on supposition of their ill tendency, is a dangerous fallacy, which at once destroys all religious liberty, because he being of course judge of that tendency will make his opinions the rule of judgment, and approve or condemn the sentiments of others only as they shall square with or differ from his own; that it is time enough for the rightful purposes of civil government, for its officers to interfere when principles break out into overt acts against peace and good order; and finally, that truth is great and will prevail if left to herself, that she is the proper and sufficient antagonist to error, and has nothing to fear from the conflict, unless by human interposition disarmed of her natural weapons, free argument and debate, errors ceasing to be dangerous when it is permitted freely to contradict them.

II. *Be it enacted by the General Assembly,* that no man shall be compelled to frequent or support any religious worship, place or ministry whatsoever, nor shall be enforced, restrained, molested, or burthened in his body or goods, nor shall otherwise suffer on account of his religious opinions or belief; but that all men shall be free to profess and by argument to maintain, their opinion in matters of religion, and that the same shall in no wise diminish, enlarge or affect their civil capacities.

III. And though we well know that this assembly, elected by the people for the ordinary purposes of legislation only, have no power to restrain the acts of succeeding assemblies, constituted with powers equal to our own, and that therefore to declare this act to be irrevocable would be of no effect in law; yet as we are free to declare, and do declare, that the rights hereby asserted are of the natural rights of mankind, and that if any act shall hereafter be passed to repeal the present, or to narrow its operation, such act will be an infringement of natural right.

VIRGINIA STATUTE OF RELIGIOUS LIBERTY

1786

I. **Facts and Concepts**

1. Look up the following words in a dictionary and write down their meanings as they are used in this document: temporal, hypocrisy, ecclesiastical, and emolument.

_____

_____

_____

_____

_____

2. According to Section I, in what manner did God create the human mind?

_____

3. In your own words, explain what the phrase "civil incapacitations" in Section I means.

_____

_____

4. According to Section I, what do attempts to limit the human mind do?

_____

_____

5. Explain the following phrase from Section I in your own words: "the Holy author of our religion, who being Lord both of body and mind, yet chose not to propagate it by coercions on either, as was in his Almighty power to do, . . . "

_____

_____

_____

6. According to Section I, what was the result of the "impious presumption of legislators, . . . setting up their own opinions . . . as the only true and infallible, . . . "?

_____

_____

7. What practice does Section I say is "sinful and tyrannical"?

_____

_____

8. What does Section I say about the relationship between civil rights and religious opinions?

_____

_____

9. Explain in your own words what it means to lay upon a citizen "an incapacity of being called to offices of trust and emolument, unless he professes or renounces this or that religious opinion . . . "

_____

_____

_____

10. According to Section I, when is the only time that public officers are justified in interfering with individual principles?

_____

_____

11. Explain in your own words the four guarantees of Section II.

_____

_____

_____

_____

_____

_____

_____

_____

12. Explain in your own words what the authors of this document say in Section III.

_____

_____

_____

II. For Further Understanding

13. What was the established church of Virginia before this statute was passed?

_____

14. Who wrote the Virginia Statute of Religious Liberty?

_____

15. This statute was one of the precedents for which amendment to the U.S. Constitution?

_____

16. This statute was passed more than a hundred years after the Maryland Toleration Act. In what important way was it an improvement over the Maryland act?

_____

_____

_____

NORTHWEST ORDINANCE

1787

The Northwest Ordinance established a badly-needed system of government for the Northwest Territory. The ordinance guaranteed the basic rights of settlers and provided for the fair treatment of Indians, the encouragement of education, and a policy of freedom rather than slavery.

An ordinance for the government of the Territory of the United States northwest of the river Ohio.

Be it ordained by the United States in Congress assembled, That the said territory, for the purposes of temporary government, be one district, subject, however, to be divided into two districts, as future circumstances may, in the opinion of Congress, make it expedient.

Be it ordained by the authority aforesaid, That the estates, both of resident and nonresident proprietors in the said territory, dying intestate, shall descend to, and be distributed among their children, and the descendants of a deceased child, in equal parts; the descendants of a deceased child or grandchild to take the share of their deceased parent in equal parts among them: And where there shall be no children or descendants, then in equal parts to the next of kin in equal degree; and among collaterals, the children of a deceased brother or sister of the intestate shall have, in equal parts among them, their deceased parents' share; and there shall in no case be a distinction between kindred of the whole and half-blood; saving, in all cases, to the widow of the intestate her third part of the real estate for life, and one-third part of the personal estate; and this law relative to descents and dower, shall remain in full force until altered by the legislature of the district. And until the governor and judges shall adopt laws as hereinafter mentioned, estates in the said territory may be devised or bequeathed by wills in writing, signed and sealed by him or her in whom the estate may be (being of full age), and attested by three witnesses; and real estates may be conveyed by lease and release, or bargain and sale, signed sealed and delivered by the person, being of full age, in whom the estate may be, and attested by two witnesses, provided such wills be duly proved, and be recorded within one year after proper magistrates, courts, and registers shall be appointed for that purpose; and personal property may be transferred by delivery; saving, however to the French and Canadian inhabitants, and other settlers of the Kaskaskies, St. Vincents and the neighboring villages who have heretofore professed themselves citizens of Virginia, their laws and customs now in force among them, relative to the descent and conveyance, of property.

Be it ordained by the authority aforesaid, That there shall be appointed from time to time by Congress, a governor, whose commission shall continue in force for the term of three years, unless sooner revoked by Congress; he shall reside in the district, and have a freehold estate therein in 1,000 acres of land, while in the exercise of his office.

There shall be appointed from time to time by Congress, a secretary, whose commission shall continue in force for four years unless sooner revoked; he shall reside in the district, and have a freehold estate therein in 500 acres of land, while in the exercise of his office. It shall be his duty to keep and preserve the acts and laws passed by the legislature, and the public records of the district, and the proceedings of the governor in his executive department, and transmit authentic copies of such acts and proceedings, every six months, to the Secretary of Congress: There shall also be appointed a court to consist of three judges, any two of whom to form a court, who shall have a common law jurisdiction, and reside in the district, and have each therein a freehold estate in 500 acres of land while in the exercise of their offices; and their commissions shall continue in force during good behavior.

The governor and judges, or a majority of them, shall adopt and publish in the district such laws of the original States, criminal and civil, as may be necessary and best suited to the circumstances of the district, and report them to Congress from time to time: which laws shall be in force in the district until the organization of the General Assembly therein, unless disapproved of by Congress; but afterwards the Legislature shall have authority to alter them as they shall think fit.

The governor, for the time being, shall be commander-in-chief of the militia, appoint and commission all officers in the same below the rank of general officers; all general officers shall be appointed and commissioned by Congress.

Previous to the organization of the general assembly, the governor shall appoint such magistrates and other civil officers in each county or township, as he shall find necessary for the preservation of the peace and good order in the same: After the general assembly shall be organized, the powers and duties of the magistrates and other civil officers shall be regulated and defined by the said assembly; but all magistrates and other civil officers not herein otherwise directed, shall, during the continuance of this temporary government, be appointed by the governor.

For the prevention of crime and injuries, the laws to be adopted or made shall have force in all parts of the district, and for the execution of process, criminal and civil, the governor shall make proper divisions thereof; and he shall proceed from time to time as circumstances may require, to lay out the parts of the district in which the Indian titles shall have been extinguished, into counties and townships, subject however to such alterations as may thereafter be made by the legislature.

So soon as there shall be five thousand free male inhabitants of full age in the district, upon giving proof thereof to the governor, they shall receive authority, with time and place, to elect representatives from their counties or townships to represent them in the general assembly: *Provided,* That, for every five hundred free male inhabitants, there shall be one representative, and so on progressively with the number of free male inhabitants shall the right of representation increase, until the number of representatives shall amount to twenty-five; after which, the number and proportion of representatives shall be regulated by the legislature: *Provided,* That no person be eligible or qualified to act as a representative unless he shall have been a citizen of one of the United States three years, and be a resident in the district, or unless he shall have resided in the district three years; and, in either case, shall likewise hold in his own right, in fee simple, two hundred acres of land within the same: *Provided, also,* That a freehold in fifty acres of land in the district, having been a citizen of one of the states, and being resident in the district, or the like freehold and two years residence in the district, shall be necessary to qualify a man as an elector of a representative.

The representatives thus elected, shall serve for the term of two years; and, in case of the death of a representative, or removal from office, the governor shall issue a writ to the county or township for which he was a member, to elect another in his stead, to serve for the residue of the term.

The general assembly or legislature shall consist of the governor, legislative council, and a house of representatives. The Legislative Council shall consist of five members, to continue in office five years, unless sooner removed by Congress; any three of whom to be a quorum: and the members of the Council shall be nominated and appointed in the following manner, to wit: As soon as representatives shall be elected, the Governor shall appoint a time and place for them to meet together; and when met, they shall nominate ten persons, residents in the district, and each possessed of a freehold in five hundred acres of land, and return their names to Congress; five of whom Congress shall appoint and commission to serve as aforesaid; and, whenever a vacancy shall happen in the council, by death or removal from office, the house of representatives shall nominate two persons, qualified as aforesaid, for each vacancy, and return their names to Congress; one of whom Congress shall appoint and commission for the residue of the term.

And every five years, four months at least before the expiration of the time of service of the members of council, the said house shall nominate ten persons, qualified as aforesaid, and return their names to Congress; five of whom Congress shall appoint and commission to serve as members of the council five years, unless sooner removed. And the governor, legislative council, and house of representatives, shall have authority to make laws in all cases, for the good government of the district, not repugnant to the principles and articles in this ordinance established and declared. And all bills, having passed by a majority in the house, and by a majority in the council, shall be referred to the governor for his assent; but no bill or legislative act whatever, shall be of any force without his assent. The governor shall have power to convene, prorogue, and dissolve the general assembly, when, in his opinion, it shall be expedient.

The governor, judges, legislative council, secretary, and such other officers as Congress shall appoint in the district, shall take an oath or affirmation of fidelity and of office; the governor before the president of congress, and all other officers before the Governor. As soon as a legislature shall be formed in the district, the council and house assembled in one room, shall have authority, by joint ballot, to elect a delegate to Congress, who shall have a seat in Congress, with a right of debating but not of voting during this temporary government.

And, for extending the fundamental principles of civil and religious liberty, which form the basis whereon these republics, their laws and constitutions are erected; to fix and establish those principles as the basis of all laws, constitutions, and governments, which forever hereafter shall be formed in the said territory: To provide also for the establishment of States, and permanent government therein, and for their admission to a share in the federal councils on an equal footing with the original States, at as early periods as may be consistent with the general interest.

It is hereby ordained and declared by the authority aforesaid, That the following articles shall be considered as articles of compact between the original States and the people and States in the said territory and forever remain unalterable, unless by common consent, to wit:

Article 1. No person, demeaning himself in a peaceable and orderly manner, shall ever be molested on account of his mode of worship or religious sentiments, in the said territory.

Article 2. The inhabitants of the said territory shall always be entitled to the benefits of the writ of *habeas corpus,* and of the trial by jury; of a proportionate representation of the people in the legislature; and of judicial proceedings according to the course of the common law. All persons shall be bailable, unless for capital offences, where the proof shall be evident or the presumption great. All fines shall be moderate; and no cruel or unusual punishments shall be inflicted. No man shall be deprived of his liberty or property, but by the judgment of his peers or the law of the land; and should the public exigencies make it necessary, for the common preservation, to take any person's property, or to demand his particular services, full compensation shall be made for the same. And in the just preservation of rights and property, it is understood and declared, that no law ought ever to be made, or have force in the said territory, that shall, in any manner whatever, interfere with or affect private contracts or engagements, *bona fide,* and without fraud, previously formed.

Article 3. Religion, morality, and knowledge, being necessary to good government and the happiness of mankind, schools and the means of education shall forever be encouraged. The utmost good faith shall always be observed towards the Indians; their lands and property shall never be taken from them without their consent; and in their property, rights, and liberty, they shall never be invaded or disturbed, unless in just and lawful wars authorized by Congress; but laws founded in justice and humanity, shall from time to time be made for preventing wrongs being done to them, and for preserving peace and friendship with them.

Article 4. The said territory, and the States which may be formed therein, shall forever remain a part of this Confederacy of the United States of America, subject to the Articles of Confederation, and to such alterations therein as shall be constitutionally made; and to all the acts and ordinances of the United States in Congress assembled, conformable thereto. The inhabitants and settlers in the said territory shall be subject to pay a part of the federal debts contracted or to be contracted, and a proportional part of the expenses of government, to be apportioned on them by Congress according to the same common rule and measure by which apportionments thereof shall be made on the other States; and the taxes for paying their proportion shall be laid and levied by the authority and direction of the legislatures of the district or districts, or new States, as in the original States, within the time agreed upon by the United States in Congress assembled. The legislatures of those districts or new States, shall never interfere with the primary disposal of the soil by the United States in Congress assembled, nor with any regulations Congress may find necessary for securing the title in such soil to the *bona fide* purchasers. No tax shall be imposed on lands the property of the United States; and, in no case, shall non-resident proprietors be taxed higher than residents. The navigable waters leading into the Mississippi and St. Lawrence, and the carrying places between the same, shall be common highways and forever free, as well to the inhabitants of the said territory as to the citizens of the United States, and those of any other States that may be admitted into the confederacy, without any tax, impost, or duty therefor.

Article 5. There shall be formed in the said territory, not less than three nor more than five States; and the boundaries of the States, as soon as Virginia shall alter her act of cession, and consent to the same, shall become fixed and established as follows, to wit: The western State in the said territory, shall be bounded by the Mississippi, the Ohio, and Wabash Rivers; a direct line drawn from the Wabash and Post Vincents, due North, to the territorial line between the United States and Canada; and, by the said territorial line, to the Lake of the Woods and Mississippi. The middle State shall be bounded by the said direct line, the Wabash from Post Vincents to the Ohio, by the Ohio, by a direct line, drawn due north from the mouth of the Great Miami, to the said territorial line, and by the said territorial line. The eastern State shall be bounded by the last mentioned direct line, the Ohio, Pennsylvania, and the said territorial line: *Provided, however,* and it is further understood and declared, that the boundaries of these three States shall be subject so far to be altered, that, if Congress shall hereafter find it expedient, they shall have authority to form one or two States in that part of the said territory which lies north of an east and west line drawn through the southerly bend or extreme of lake Michigan. And, whenever any of the said States shall have sixty thousand free inhabitants therein, such State shall be admitted, by its delegates, into the Congress of the United States, on an equal footing with the original States in all respects whatever, and shall be at liberty to form a permanent constitution and State government: *Provided,* the constitution and government so to be formed, shall be republican, and in conformity to the principles contained in these articles; and, so far as it can be consistent with the general interest of the confederacy, such admission shall be allowed at an earlier period, and when there may be a less number of free inhabitants in the State than sixty thousand.

Article 6. There shall be neither slavery nor involuntary servitude in the said territory, otherwise than in the punishment of crimes whereof the party shall have been duly convicted: *Provided, always,* That any person escaping into the same, from whom labor or service is lawfully claimed in any one of the original States, such fugitive may be lawfully reclaimed and conveyed to the person claiming his or her labor or service as aforesaid.

Be it ordained by the authority aforesaid, That the resolutions of the 23rd of April 1784, relative to the subject of this ordinance, be, and the same are hereby repealed and declared null and void.

NORTHWEST ORDINANCE
1787

I. Facts and Concepts

1. What was the geographical location of the territory governed by this ordinance?

   _____

2. Who appointed the governor of the territory? How long was the governor's term?

   _____

   _____

3. Who appointed the secretary of the territory? What were the secretary's duties?

   _____

   _____

   _____

4. How many judges were appointed to the territory?

   _____

5. Who was designated to provide laws for the territory until a general assembly could be organized?

   _____

6. Read the paragraph that begins, "So soon as there shall be . . . " and answer the following questions.

   a. How many free males had to live in the district before the general assembly could be formed?

   _____

   b. Each representative in the legislature represented how many free males?

   _____

   c. When did the legislature begin regulating the number and proportion of representatives?

   _____

d. What qualifications did a person have to meet in order to be elected a representative?

_____

_____

_____

e. What qualifications did a person have to meet in order to elect representatives?

_____

_____

_____

7. Read the paragraph that begins, "The general assembly . . ." and answer the following questions.

a. What three people or bodies made up the legislature?

_____

b. How many members were on the legislative council and how long were their terms in office?

_____

c. How were the members of the legislative council chosen?

_____

_____

_____

_____

d. Did the governor have the right to veto bills? Give a quotation from the paragraph to support your answer.

_____

_____

_____

_____

e. Look up the word "prorogue" in a dictionary or history book and write down its definition. What three powers, besides the right of veto, did the governor have over the legislature?

_____

_____

_____

8. Read the paragraph that begins, "The governor, judges, legislative council, . . . " and answer the following questions.

a. How was the territory's representative to Congress chosen?

_____

_____

_____

b. Describe this representative's role in Congress.

_____

_____

9. The paragraph that begins, "And, for extending . . . " discusses the formation of states out of the territory. Quote a phrase from this paragraph describing the status of these states in comparison with the original thirteen states.

_____

_____

_____

10. State in your own words the guarantee of Article 1.

_____

_____

11. List three rights granted to the residents of the territory in Article 2.

_____

_____

_____

12. Read Article 3 and answer the following questions.

    a. What is encouraged at the beginning of this article? Why?

_____

_____

    b. What Indian policy is encouraged in this article?

_____

_____

_____

13. Read Article 5 and answer the following questions.

    a. How many states were to be formed out of this territory?

_____

    b. What is the only requirement for statehood listed in this article?

_____

    c. What requirement does this article make about new state governments?

_____

14. Read Article 6 and answer the following questions.

    a. Was slavery allowed in the Northwest Territory? Give a quotation from this article to support your answer.

_____

_____

b. State the main idea of the part of this article that begins *Provided, always*, in your own words.

_____

_____

_____

II. For Further Understanding

15. This document says that "the legislatures of those districts or new States, shall never interfere with the primary disposal of the soil by the United States in Congress assembled." That refers to what law passed in 1785 concerning the sale of land in the Northwest Territory?

_____

16. What states were carved out of the Northwest Territory?

_____

17. Do property requirements for voting or holding office still exist in the United States?

_____

18. Under the U.S. Constitution, does the president have the power to convene, prorogue, or dissolve Congress?

_____

_____

_____

THE FEDERALIST, NO. 10

by James Madison

1787

The writing and signing of the U.S. Constitution was a huge task, but an even greater struggle came later when the Constitution was sent to the states for ratification. Opponents and supporters of the Constitution argued about it in every state. Among the supporters were the authors of **The Federalist:** *Alexander Hamilton, James Madison, and John Jay.* **The Federalist** *was originally written to convince New Yorkers to ratify the Constitution, but it has since become one of the most important works of American political theory.*

Among the numerous advantages promised by a well-constructed Union, none deserves to be more accurately developed than its tendency to break and control the violence of faction. The friend of popular governments never finds himself so much alarmed for their character and fate as when he contemplates their propensity to this dangerous vice. He will not fail, therefore, to set a due value on any plan which, without violating the principles to which he is attached, provides a proper cure for it. The instability, injustice, and confusion introduced into the public councils have, in truth, been the mortal diseases under which popular governments have everywhere perished, as they continue to be the favorite and fruitful topics from which the adversaries to liberty derive their most specious declamations. The valuable improvements made by the American constitutions on the popular models, both ancient and modern, cannot certainly be too much admired; but it would be an unwarrantable partiality to contend that they have as effectually obviated the danger on this side, as was wished and expected. Complaints are everywhere heard from our most considerate and virtuous citizens, equally the friends of public and private faith and of public and personal liberty, that our governments are too unstable, that the public good is disregarded in the conflicts of rival parties, and that measures are too often decided, not according to the rules of justice and the rights of the minor party, but by the superior force of an interested and overbearing majority. However anxiously we may wish that these complaints had no foundation, the evidence of known facts will not permit us to deny that they are in some degree true. It will be found, indeed, on a candid review of our situation, that some of the distresses under which we labor have been erroneously charged on the operation of our governments; but it will be found, at the same time, that other causes will not alone account for many of our heaviest misfortunes; and particularly, for that prevailing and increasing distrust of public engagements and alarm for private rights which are echoed from one end of the continent to the other. These must be chiefly, if not wholly, effects of the unsteadiness and injustice with which a factious spirit has tainted our public administration.

By a faction I understand a number of citizens, whether amounting to a majority or minority of the whole, who are united and actuated by some common impulse of passion, or of interest, adverse to the rights of other citizens, or to the permanent and aggregate interests of the community.

There are two methods of curing the mischiefs of faction: the one, by removing its causes; the other, by controlling its effects.

There are again two methods of removing the causes of faction: the one, by destroying the liberty which is essential to its existence; the other, by giving to every citizen the same opinions, the same passions, and the same interests.

It could never be more truly said than of the first remedy that it was worse than the disease. Liberty is to faction what air is to fire, an aliment without which it instantly expires. But it could not be a less folly to abolish liberty, which is essential to political life, because it nourishes faction than it would be to wish the annihilation of air, which is essential to animal life, because it imparts to fire its destructive agency.

The second expedient is as impracticable as the first would be unwise. As long as the reason of man continues fallible, and he is at liberty to exercise it, different opinions will be formed. As long as the connection subsists between his reason and his self-love, his opinions and his passions will have a reciprocal influence on each other; and the former will be objects to which the latter will attach themselves. The diversity in the faculties of men, from which the rights of property originate, is not less than an insuperable obstacle to a uniformity of interests. The protection of these faculties is the first object of government. From the protection of different and unequal faculties of acquiring property, the possession of different degrees and kinds of property immediately results; and from the influence of these on the sentiments and views of the respective proprietors ensues a division of the society into different interests and parties.

The latent causes of faction are thus sown in the nature of man; and we see them everywhere brought into different degrees of activity, according to the different circumstances of civil society. A zeal for different opinions concerning religion, concerning government, and many other points, as well of speculation as of practice; an attachment to different leaders ambitiously contending for pre-eminence and power; or to persons of other descriptions whose fortunes have been interesting to the human passions, have, in turn, divided mankind into parties, inflamed them with mutual animosity, and rendered them much more disposed to vex and oppress each other than to co-operate for their common good. So strong is this propensity of mankind to fall into mutual animosities that where no substantial occasion presents itself the most frivolous and fanciful distinctions have been sufficient to kindle their unfriendly passions and excite their most violent conflicts. But the most common and durable source of factions has been the verious and unequal distribution of property. Those who hold and those who are without property have ever formed distinct interests in society. Those who are creditors, and those who are debtors, fall under a like discrimination. A landed interest, a manufacturing interest, a mercantile interest, a moneyed interest, with many lesser interests, grow up of necessity in civilized nations, and divide them into different classes, actuated by different sentiments and views. The regulation of these various and interfering interests forms the principal task of modern legislation and involves the spirit of party and faction in the necessary and ordinary operations of government . . .

The inference to which we are brought is that the *causes* of faction cannot be removed and that relief is only to be sought in the means of controlling its *effects*.

If a faction consists of less than a majority, relief is supplied by the republican principle, which enables the majority to defeat its sinister views by regular vote. It may clog the administration, it may convulse the society; but it will be unable to execute and mask its violence under the forms of the Constitution. When a majority is included in a faction, the form of popular government, on the other hand, enables it to sacrifice to its ruling passion or interest both the public good and the rights of other citizens. To secure the public good and private rights against the danger of such a faction, and at the same time to preserve the spirit and the form of popular government, is then the great object to which our inquiries are directed. Let me add that it is the great desideratum by which alone this form of government can be rescued from the opprobrium under which it has so long labored and be recommended to the esteem and adoption of mankind.

By what means is this object attainable? Evidently by one of two only. Either the existence of the same passion or interest in a majority at the same time must be prevented, or the majority, having such coexistent passion or interest, must be rendered, by their number and local situation, unable to concert and carry into effect schemes of oppression. If the impulse and the opportunity be suffered to coincide, we well know that neither moral nor religious motives can be relied on as an adequate control. They are not found to be such on the injustice and violence of individuals, and lose their efficacy in proportion to the number combined together, that is, in proportion as their efficacy becomes needful.

From this view of the subject it may be concluded that a pure democracy, by which I mean a society consisting of a small number of citizens, who assemble and administer the government in person, can admit of no cure for the mischiefs of faction. A common passion or interest will, in almost every case, be felt by a majority of the whole; a communication and concert results from the form of government itself; and there is nothing to check the inducements to sacrifice the weaker party or an obnoxious individual. Hence it is that such democracies have ever been spectacles of turbulence and contention; have ever been found incompatible with personal security or the rights of property; and have in general been as short in their lives as they have been violent in their deaths. Theoretic politicians, who have patronized this species of government, have erroneously supposed that by reducing mankind to a perfect equality in their political rights, they would at the same time be perfectly equalized and assimilated in their possessions, their opinions, and their passions.

A republic, by which I mean a government in which the scheme of representation takes place, opens a different prospect and promises the cure for which we are seeking. Let us examine the points in which it varies from pure democracy, and we shall comprehend both the nature of the cure and the efficacy which it must derive from the Union.

The two great points of

difference between a democracy and a republic are: first, the delegation of government in the latter, to a small number of citizens elected by the rest; secondly, the greater number of citizens and greater sphere of country over which the latter may be extended.

The effect of the first difference is, on the one hand, to refine and enlarge the public views by passing them through the medium of the chosen body of citizens, whose wisdom may best determine the true interest of their country and whose patriotism and love of justice will be least likely to sacrifice it to temporary or partial considerations. Under such a regulation it may well happen that the public voice, pronounced by the representatives of people, will be more consonant to the public good than if pronounced by the people themselves, convened for the purpose . . .

The other point of difference is the greater number of citizens and extent of territory which may be brought within the compass of republican than of democratic government; and it is this circumstance principally which renders factious combinations less to be dreaded in the former than in the latter. The smaller the society, the fewer will be the distinct parties and interests composing it; the fewer the distinct parties and interests, the more frequently will a majority be found of the same party; and the smaller the number of individuals composing a majority, and the smaller the compass within which they are placed, the more easily will they concert and execute their plans of oppression. Extend the sphere and you take in a greater variety of parties and interests; you make it less probable that a majority of the whole will have a common motive to invade the rights of other citizens; or if such a common motive exists, it will be more difficult for all who feel it to discover their own strength and to act in unison with each other. Besides other impediments, it may be remarked that, where there is a consciousness of unjust or dishonorable purposes, communication is always checked by distrust in proportion to the number whose concurrence is necessary.

Hence it clearly appears that the same advantage which a republic has over a democracy in controlling the effects of faction is enjoyed by a large over a small republic—is enjoyed by the Union over the states composing it . . .

In the extent and proper structure of the Union, therefore, we behold a republican remedy for the diseases most incident to republican government. And according to the degree of pleasure and pride we feel in being republicans ought to be our zeal in cherishing the spirit and supporting the character of federalists.

PUBLIUS

THE FEDERALIST, NO. 10
by James Madison
1787

I. Facts and Concepts

1. Read the first paragraph of the document and answer the following questions.

   a. What does Madison say is one of the greatest advantages of a "well-constructed Union"?

   _____

   b. What three things had been the "mortal diseases" of popular governments in the past?

   _____

   _____

   c. What were the three complaints "everywhere heard" about governments in the United States?

   _____

   _____

   _____

2. Look up the word "faction" in a dictionary. Then, explain in your own words Madison's definition of a faction.

   _____

   _____

   _____

3. According to Madison, what are the two ways of "curing the mischiefs of faction"?

   _____

   _____

4. According to Madison, by what two ways can the causes of faction be removed? What does he think of each of these ways?

   _____

   _____

   _____

5. In the paragraph that begins, "The latent causes of faction . . . ," what does Madison say is the "most common and durable" source of factions?

_____

_____

6. In your own words, state the conclusion Madison reaches in the paragraph that begins, "The inference to which we are brought . . . "

_____

_____

7. Read the paragraph that begins, "If a faction consists . . . " and answer the following questions.

   a. What does Madison mean by the "republican principle"?

_____

_____

   b. What happens when a majority is included in a faction?

_____

_____

8. According to the paragraph that begins, "By what means . . . " in what two ways can the danger of a majority faction be prevented?

_____

_____

_____

9. According to the paragraph that begins, "From this view . . . " can a pure democracy solve the problems of faction? Quote a phrase from the paragraph to support your answer.

_____

_____

10. How does Madison define a republic in the paragraph that begins, "A republic, . . . "?

_____

_____

11. In the paragraph that begins, "The two great . . . " what does Madison say are the two main differences between a democracy and a republic?

_____

_____

12. According to the paragraph that begins, "The other point of difference . . . " what is one advantage of a republic over a democracy?

_____

_____

13. State in your own words the main idea of the paragraph that begins, "Hence it clearly appears . . . "

_____

_____

_____

14. In one sentence of your own words, state the basic idea of this document.

_____

_____

II. For Further Understanding

15. Under what document was the United States governed at the time *The Federalist* was written?

_____

16. What were the names of the two groups that debated
    whether or not the Constitution should be ratified? On
    what main issue did they differ?

    _____

    _____

    _____

17. List three major factions in the United States today. (Hint:
    Factions today are often called special-interest groups.)

    _____

    _____

UNITED STATES CONSTITUTION

1787

The United States Constitution is one of the most important documents in world history. The framers of the Constitution turned the principles of freedom and democracy into a working government. The United States proved that this type of government could succeed, and provided a model for other nations throughout the world.

WE THE PEOPLE of the United States, in Order to form a more perfect Union, establish Justice, insure domestic Tranquility, provide for the common defence, promote the general Welfare, and secure the Blessings of Liberty to ourselves and our Posterity, do ordain and establish this Constitution for the United States of America.

ARTICLE I

SECTION 1. All legislative Powers herein granted shall be vested in a Congress of the United States, which shall consist of a Senate and House of Representatives.

SECTION 2. The House of Representatives shall be composed of Members chosen every second Year by the People of the several States, and the Electors in each State shall have the Qualifications requisite for Electors of the most numerous Branch of the State Legislature.

No Person shall be a Representative who shall not have attained to the Age of twenty five Years, and been seven Years a Citizen of the United States, and who shall not, when elected, be an Inhabitant of that State in which he shall be chosen.

Representatives and direct Taxes shall be apportioned among the several States which may be included within this Union, according to their respective Numbers, which shall be determined by adding to the whole Number of free Persons, including those bound to Service for a Term of Years, and excluding Indians not taxed, three fifths of all other Persons. The actual Enumeration shall be made within three Years after the first Meeting of the Congress of the United States, and within every subsequent Term of ten Years, in such Manner as they shall by Law direct. The Number of Representatives shall not exceed one for every thirty Thousand, but each State shall have at Least one Representative; and until such enumeration shall be made, the State of New Hampshire shall be entitled to chuse three, Massachusetts eight, Rhode-Island and Providence Plantations one, Connecticut five, New-York six, New Jersey four, Pennsylvania eight, Delaware one, Maryland six, Virginia ten, North Carolina five, South Carolina five, and Georgia three.

When vacancies happen in the Representation from any State, the Executive Authority thereof shall issue Writs of Election to fill such Vacancies.

The House of Representatives shall chuse their Speaker and other Officers; and shall have the sole Power of Impeachment.

SECTION 3. The Senate of the United States shall be composed of two Senators from each State, chosen by the Legislature thereof, for six Years; and each Senator shall have one Vote.

Immediately after they shall be assembled in Consequence of the first Election, they shall be divided as equally as may be into three Classes. The Seats of the

Senators of the first Class shall be vacated at the Expiration of the second Year, of the second Class at the Expiration of the fourth Year, and of the third Class at the Expiration of the sixth Year, so that one third may be chosen every second Year; and if Vacancies happen by Resignation, or otherwise, during the Recess of the Legislature of any State, the Executive thereof may make temporary Appointments until the next Meeting of the Legislature, which shall then fill such Vacancies.

No Person shall be a Senator who shall not have attained to the Age of thirty Years, and been nine Years a Citizen of the United States, and who shall not, when elected, be an Inhabitant of that State for which he shall be chosen.

The Vice President of the United States shall be President of the Senate, but shall have no Vote, unless they be equally divided.

The Senate shall chuse their other Officers, and also a President pro tempore, in the Absence of the Vice President, or when he shall exercise the Office of President of the United States.

The Senate shall have the sole Power to try all Impeachments. When sitting for that Purpose, they shall be on Oath or Affirmation. When the President of the United States is tried, the Chief Justice shall preside: And no Person shall be convicted without the Concurrence of two thirds of the Members present.

Judgment in Cases of Impeachment shall not extend further than to removal from Office, and disqualification to hold and enjoy any Office of honor, Trust or Profit under the United States: but the Party convicted shall nevertheless be liable and subject to Indictment, Trial, Judgment and Punishment, according to Law.

SECTION 4. The Times, Places and Manner of holding Elections for Senators and Representatives, shall be prescribed in each State by the Legislature thereof; but the Congress may at any time by Law make or alter such Regulations, except as to the Places of chusing Senators.

The Congress shall assemble at least once in every Year, and such Meeting shall be on the first Monday in December, unless they shall by Law appoint a different Day.

SECTION 5. Each House shall be the Judge of the Elections, Returns and Qualifications of its own Members, and a Majority of each shall constitute a Quorum to do Business; but a smaller Number may adjourn from day to day, and may be authorized to compel the Attendance of absent Members, in such Manner, and under such Penalties as each House may provide.

Each House may determine the Rules of its Proceedings, punish its Members for disorderly Behaviour, and with the Concurrence of two thirds, expel a Member.

Each House shall keep a Journal of its Proceedings, and from time to time publish the same, excepting such Parts as may in their Judgment require Secrecy; and the Yeas and Nays of the Members of either House on any question shall, at the Desire of one fifth of those Present, be entered on the Journal.

Neither House, during the Session of Congress, shall, without the Consent of the other, adjourn for more than three days, nor to any other Place than that in which the two Houses shall be sitting.

SECTION 6. The Senators and Representatives shall receive a Compensation for their Services, to be ascertained by Law, and paid out of the Treasury of the United States. They shall in all Cases, except Treason, Felony and Breach of the Peace, be privileged from Arrest during their Attendance at the Session of their respective Houses, and in going to and returning from the same; and for any Speech or Debate in either House, they shall not be questioned in any other Place.

No Senator or Representative shall, during the Time for which he was elected, be appointed to any civil Office under the Authority of the United States which shall have been created, or the Emoluments whereof shall have been encreased during such time; and no Person holding any Office under the United States, shall be a Member of either House during his Continuance in Office.

SECTION 7. All Bills for raising Revenue shall originate in the House of Representatives; but the Senate may propose or concur with Amendments as on other Bills.

Every Bill which shall have passed the House of Representatives and the Senate, shall, before it become a Law, be presented to the President of the United States; If he approve he shall sign it, but if not he shall return it, with his Objections to that House in which it shall have originated, who shall enter the Objections at large on their Journal, and proceed to reconsider it. If after such Reconsideration two thirds of that House shall agree to pass the Bill, it shall be sent, together with the Objections, to the other House,

by which it shall likewise be reconsidered, and if approved by two thirds of that House, it shall become a Law. But in all such Cases the Votes of both Houses shall be determined by yeas and Nays, and the Names of the Persons voting for and against the Bill shall be entered on the Journal of each House respectively. If any Bill shall not be returned by the President within ten Days (Sundays excepted) after it shall have been presented to him, the Same shall be a Law, in like Manner as if he had signed it, unless the Congress by their Adjournment prevent its Return, in which Case it shall not be a Law.

Every Order, Resolution, or Vote to which the Concurrence of the Senate and House of Representatives may be necessary (except on a question of Adjournment) shall be presented to the President of the United States; and before the Same shall take Effect, shall be approved by him, or being disapproved by him, shall be repassed by two thirds of the Senate and House of Representatives, according to the Rules and Limitations prescribed in the Case of a Bill.

SECTION 8. The Congress shall have Power To lay and collect Taxes, Duties, Imposts and Excises, to pay the Debts and provide for the common Defence and general Welfare of the United States; but all Duties, Imposts and Excises shall be uniform throughout the United States;

To borrow Money on the credit of the United States;

To regulate Commerce with foreign Nations, and among the several States, and with the Indian Tribes;

To establish an uniform Rule of Naturalization, and uniform

Laws on the subject of Bankruptcies throughout the United States;

To coin Money, regulate the Value thereof, and of foreign Coin, and fix the Standard of Weights and Measures;

To provide for the Punishment of counterfeiting the Securities and current Coin of the United States;

To establish Post Offices and post Roads;

To promote the Progress of Science and useful Arts, by securing for limited Times to Authors and Inventors the exclusive Right to their respective Writings and Discoveries;

To constitute Tribunals inferior to the supreme Court;

To define and punish Piracies and Felonies committed on the high Seas, and Offences against the Law of Nations;

To declare War, grant Letters of Marque and Reprisal, and make Rules concerning Captures on Land and Water;

To raise and support Armies, but no Appropriation of Money to that Use shall be for a longer Term than two Years;

To provide and maintain a Navy;

To make Rules for the Government and Regulation of the land and naval Forces;

To provide for calling forth the Militia to execute the Laws of the Union, suppress Insurrections and repel Invasions;

To provide for organizing, arming, and disciplining, the Militia, and for governing such Part of them as may be employed in the Service of the United States, reserving to the States respectively, the Appointment of the Officers, and the Authority of training the Militia according to the discipline prescribed by Congress;

To exercise exclusive Legislation in all Cases whatsoever, over such District (not exceeding ten Miles square) as may, by Cession of particular States, and the Acceptance of Congress, become the Seat of the Government of the United States, and to exercise like Authority over all Places purchased by the Consent of the Legislature of the State in which the Same shall be, for the Erection of Forts, Magazines, Arsenals, dock-Yards, and other needful Buildings; And—

To make all Laws which shall be necessary and proper for carrying into Execution the foregoing Powers, and all other Powers vested by this Constitution in the Government of the United States, or in any Department or Officer thereof.

SECTION 9. The Migration or Importation of such Persons as any of the States now existing shall think proper to admit, shall not be prohibited by the Congress prior to the Year one thousand eight hundred and eight, but a Tax or duty may be imposed on such Importation, not exceeding ten dollars for each Person.

The Privilege of the Writ of Habeas Corpus shall not be suspended, unless when in Cases of Rebellion or Invasion the public Safety may require it.

No Bill of Attainder or ex post facto Law shall be passed.

No Capitation, or other direct, Tax shall be laid, unless in Proportion to the Census or Enumeration herein before directed to be taken.

No Tax or Duty shall be laid on Articles exported from any State.

No Preference shall be given by any Regulation of Commerce or Revenue to the Ports of one State over those of another: nor shall Vessels bound to, or from, one

State, be obliged to enter, clear, or pay Duties in another.

No Money shall be drawn from the Treasury, but in Consequence of Appropriations made by Law; and a regular Statement and Account of the Receipts and Expenditures of all public Money shall be published from time to time.

No Title of Nobility shall be granted by the United States: And no Person holding any Office of Profit or Trust under them, shall, without the Consent of the Congress, accept of any present, Emolument, Office, or Title, of any kind whatever, from any King, Prince or foreign State.

SECTION 10. No State shall enter into any Treaty, Alliance, or Confederation; grant Letters of Marque and Reprisal; coin Money; emit Bills of Credit; make any Thing but gold and silver Coin a Tender in Payment of Debts; pass any Bill of Attainder, ex post facto Law, or Law impairing the Obligation of Contracts, or grant any Title of Nobility.

No State shall, without the Consent of the Congress, lay any Imposts or Duties on Imports or Exports, except what may be absolutely necessary for executing it's inspection Laws: and the net Produce of all Duties and Imposts, laid by any State on Imports or Exports, shall be for the Use of the Treasury of the United States; and all such Laws shall be subject to the Revision and Controul of the Congress.

No State shall, without the Consent of Congress, lay any Duty of Tonnage, keep Troops, or Ships of War in time of Peace, enter into any Agreement or Compact with another State, or with a foreign Power, or engage in War, unless actually invaded, or in such

imminent Danger as will not admit of delay.

ARTICLE II

SECTION 1. The executive Power shall be vested in a President of the United States of America. He shall hold his Office during the Term of four Years, and, together with the Vice President, chosen for the same Term, be elected, as follows

Each State shall appoint, in such Manner as the Legislature thereof may direct, a Number of Electors, equal to the whole Number of Senators and Representatives to which the State may be entitled in the Congress: but no Senator or Representative, or Person holding an Office of Trust or Profit under the United States, shall be appointed an Elector.

The Electors shall meet in their respective States, and vote by Ballot for two Persons, of whom one at least shall not be an Inhabitant of the same State with themselves. And they shall make a List of all the Persons voted for, and of the Number of Votes for each; which List they shall sign and certify, and transmit sealed to the Seat of the Government of the United States, directed to the President of the Senate. The President of the Senate shall, in the Presence of the Senate and House of Representatives, open all the Certificates, and the Votes shall then be counted. The Person having the greatest Number of Votes shall be the President, if such Number be a Majority of the whole Number of Electors appointed; and if there be more than one who have such Majority, and have an equal Number of Votes, then the House of Representatives shall immediately chuse by Ballot one of them for President; and if no person have a Majority, then from the five highest on the List the said House shall in like Manner chuse the President. But in chusing the President, the Votes shall be taken by States, the Representation from each State having one Vote; A quorum for this Purpose shall consist of a Member or Members from two thirds of the States, and a Majority of all the States shall be necessary to a Choice. In every Case, after the Choice of the President, the Person having the greatest Number of Votes of the Electors shall be the Vice President. But if there should remain two or more who have equal Votes, the Senate shall chuse from them by Ballot the Vice President.

The Congress may determine the Time of chusing the Electors, and the Day on which they shall give their Votes; which Day shall be the same throughout the United States.

No Person except a natural born Citizen, or a Citizen of the United States, at the time of the Adoption of this Constitution, shall be eligible to the Office of President; neither shall any Person be eligible to that Office who shall not have attained to the Age of thirty five Years, and been fourteen Years a Resident within the United States.

In Case of the Removal of the President from Office, or of his Death, Resignation, or Inability to discharge the Powers and Duties of the said Office, the Same shall devolve on the Vice President, and the Congress may by Law provide for the Case of Removal, Death, Resignation or Inability, both of the President and Vice President, declaring what Officer shall then act as President, and such Officer shall act accordingly, until the Disability be removed, or a

President shall be elected.

The President shall, at stated Times, receive for his Services, a Compensation, which shall neither be encreased nor diminished during the Period for which he shall have been elected, and he shall not receive within that Period any other Emolument from the United States, or any of them.

Before he enter on the Execution of his Office, he shall take the following Oath or Affirmation:—"I do solemnly swear (or affirm) that I will faithfully execute the Office of President of the United States, and will to the best of my Ability, preserve, protect and defend the Constitution of the United States."

SECTION 2. The President shall be Commander in Chief of the Army and Navy of the United States, and of the Militia of the several States, when called into the actual Service of the United States; he may require the Opinion, in writing, of the principal Officer in each of the executive Departments, upon any Subject relating to the Duties of their respective Offices, and he shall have Power to grant Reprieves and Pardons for Offences against the United States, except in Cases of Impeachment.

He shall have Power, by and with the Advice and Consent of the Senate, to make Treaties, provided two thirds of the Senators present concur; and he shall nominate, and by and with the Advice and Consent of the Senate, shall appoint Ambassadors, other public Ministers and Consuls, Judges of the supreme Court, and all other Officers of the United States, whose Appointments are not herein otherwise provided for, and which shall be established by Law: but the Congress may by

93

Law vest the Appointment of such inferior Officers, as they think proper, in the President alone, in the Courts of Law, or in the Heads of Departments.

The President shall have Power to fill up all Vacancies that may happen during the Recess of the Senate, by granting Commissions which shall expire at the End of their next Session.

SECTION 3. He shall from time to time give to the Congress Information of the State of the Union, and recommend to their Consideration such Measures as he shall judge necessary and expedient; he may, on extraordinary Occasions, convene both Houses, or either of them, and in Case of Disagreement between them, with Respect to the Time of Adjournment, he may adjourn them to such Time as he shall think proper; he shall receive Ambassadors and other public Ministers; he shall take Care that the Laws be faithfully executed, and shall Commission all the Officers of the United States.

SECTION 4. The President, Vice President and all civil Officers of the United States, shall be removed from Office on Impeachment for, and Conviction of, Treason, Bribery, or other high Crimes and Misdemeanors.

ARTICLE III

SECTION 1. The judicial Power of the United States, shall be vested in one supreme Court, and in such inferior Courts as the Congress may from time to time ordain and establish. The Judges, both of the supreme and inferior Courts, shall hold their Offices during good Behaviour, and shall, at stated Times, receive for their Services, a Compensation, which shall not be diminished during their Continuance in Office.

SECTION 2. The judicial Power shall extend to all Cases, in Law and Equity, arising under this Constitution, the Laws of the United States, and Treaties made, or which shall be made, under their Authority;—to all Cases affecting Ambassadors, other public Ministers and Consuls;—to all Cases of admiralty and maritime Jurisdiction;—to Controversies to which the United States shall be a Party;—to Controversies between two or more States;—between a State and Citizens of another State;—between Citizens of different States,—between Citizens of the same State claiming Lands under Grants of different States, and between a State, or the Citizens thereof, and foreign States, Citizens or Subjects.

In all Cases affecting Ambassadors, other public Ministers and Consuls, and those in which a State shall be Party, the supreme Court shall have original Jurisdiction. In all the other Cases before mentioned, the supreme Court shall have appellate Jurisdiction, both as to Law and Fact, with such Exceptions, and under such Regulations as the Congress shall make.

The Trial of all Crimes, except in Cases of Impeachment, shall be by Jury; and such Trial shall be held in the State where the said Crimes shall have been committed; but when not committed within any State, the Trial shall be at such Place or Places as the Congress may by Law have directed.

SECTION 3. Treason against the United States, shall consist only in levying War against them, or in adhering to their Enemies, giving them Aid and Comfort. No Person shall be convicted of Treason unless on the Testimony of two Witnesses to the same overt Act, or on Confession in open Court.

The Congress shall have Power to declare the Punishment of Treason, but no Attainder of Treason shall work Corruption of Blood, or Forfeiture except during the Life of the Person attainted.

ARTICLE IV

SECTION 1. Full Faith and Credit shall be given in each State to the Public Acts, Records, and judicial Proceedings of every other State. And the Congress may by general Laws prescribe the Manner in which such Acts, Records and Proceedings shall be proved, and the Effect thereof.

SECTION 2. The Citizens of each State shall be entitled to all Privileges and Immunities of Citizens in the several States.

A Person charged in any State with Treason, Felony, or other Crime, who shall flee from Justice, and be found in another State, shall on Demand of the executive Authority of the State from which he fled, be delivered up, to be removed to the State having Jurisdiction of the Crime.

No Person held to Service or Labour in one State, under the Laws thereof, escaping into another, shall, in Consequence of any Law or Regulation therein, be discharged from such Service or Labour, but shall be delivered up on Claim of the Party to whom such Service or Labour may be due.

SECTION 3. New States may be admitted by the Congress into this Union; but no new States shall be formed or erected within the Jurisdiction of any other State;

nor any State be formed by the Junction of two or more States, or Parts of States, without the Consent of the Legislatures of the States concerned as well as of the Congress.

The Congress shall have Power to dispose of and make all needful Rules and Regulations respecting the Territory or other Property belonging to the United States; and nothing in this Constitution shall be so construed as to Prejudice any Claims of the United States, or of any particular State.

SECTION 4. The United States shall guarantee to every State in this Union a Republican form of Government, and shall protect each of them against Invasion; and on Application of the Legislature, or of the Executive (when the Legislature cannot be convened) against domestic Violence.

ARTICLE V

The Congress, whenever two thirds of both Houses shall deem it necessary, shall propose Amendments to this Constitution, or, on the Application of the Legislatures of two thirds of the several States, shall call a Convention for proposing Amendments, which, in either Case, shall be valid to all Intents and Purposes, as Part of this Constitution, when ratified by the Legislatures of three fourths of the several States, or by Conventions in three fourths thereof, as the one or the other Mode of Ratification may be proposed by the Congress; Provided that no Amendment which may be made prior to the Year One thousand eight hundred and eight shall in any Manner affect the first and fourth Clauses in the Ninth Section of the first Article; and that no State, without its Consent, shall be deprived of it's equal Suffrage in the Senate.

ARTICLE VI

All Debts contracted and Engagements entered into, before the Adoption of this Constitution, shall be as valid against the United States under this Constitution, as under the Confederation.

This Constitution, and the Laws of the United States which shall be made in Pursuance thereof; and all Treaties made, or which shall be made, under the Authority of the United States, shall be the supreme Law of the Land; and the Judges in every State shall be bound thereby, any Thing in the Constitution or Laws of any State to the Contrary notwithstanding.

The Senators and Representatives before mentioned, and the Members of the several State Legislatures, and all executive and judicial Officers, both of the United States and of the several States, shall be bound by Oath or Affirmation, to support this Constitution; but no religious Test shall ever be required as a Qualification to any Office or public Trust under the United States.

ARTICLE VII

The Ratification of the Conventions of nine States, shall be sufficient for the Establishment of this Constitution between the States so ratifying the Same.

DONE in Convention by the Unanimous Consent of the States present the Seventeenth Day of September in the Year of our Lord one thousand seven hundred and Eighty seven and of the Independence of the United States

of America the Twelfth. IN WITNESS whereof We have hereunto subscribed our Names.

THE BILL OF RIGHTS
1791

ARTICLE I

Congress shall make no law respecting an establishment of religion, or prohibiting the free exercise thereof; or abridging the freedom of speech, or of the press; or the right of the people peaceably to assemble, and to petition the government for a redress of grievances.

ARTICLE II

A well regulated Militia, being necessary to the security of a free State, the right of the people to keep and bear Arms, shall not be infringed.

ARTICLE III

No Soldier shall, in time of peace be quartered in any house, without the consent of the Owner, nor in time of war, but in a manner to be prescribed by law.

ARTICLE IV

The right of the people to be secure in their persons, houses, papers, and effects, against unreasonable searches and seizures, shall not be violated, and no Warrants shall issue, but upon probable cause, supported by Oath or affirmation, and particularly describing the place to be searched, and the persons or things to be seized.

ARTICLE V

No person shall be held to answer for a capital, or otherwise infamous crime, unless on a presentment or indictment of a Grand Jury, except in cases arising in the land or naval forces, or in the Militia, when in actual service in time of War or public danger; nor shall any person be subject for the same offence to be twice put in jeopardy of life or limb; nor shall be compelled in any criminal case to be a witness against himself, nor be deprived of life, liberty, or property, without due process of law; nor shall private property be taken for public use, without just compensation.

ARTICLE VI

In all criminal prosecutions, the accused shall enjoy the right to a speedy and public trial, by an impartial jury of the State and district wherein the crime shall have been committed, which district shall have been previously ascertained by law, and to be informed of the nature and cause of the accusation; to be confronted with the witnesses against him; to have compulsory process for obtaining witnesses in his favor, and to have the Assistance of Counsel for his defence.

ARTICLE VII

In Suits at common law, where the value in controversy shall exceed twenty dollars, the right of trial by jury shall be preserved, and no fact tried by a jury, shall be otherwise re-examined in any Court of the United States, than according to the rules of the common law.

ARTICLE VIII

Excessive bail shall not be required, nor excessive fines imposed, nor cruel and unusual punishments inflicted.

ARTICLE IX

The enumeration in the Constitution, of certain rights, shall not be construed to deny or disparage others retained by the people.

ARTICLE X

The powers not delegated to the United States by the Constitution, nor prohibited by it to the States, are reserved to the States respectively, or to the people.

OTHER AMENDMENTS

ARTICLE XI
1798

The Judicial power of the United States shall not be construed to extend to any suit in law or equity, commenced or prosecuted against one of the United States by Citizens of another State, or by Citizens or Subjects of any Foreign State.

ARTICLE XII
1804

The Electors shall meet in their respective states, and vote by ballot for President and Vice-President, one of whom, at least, shall not be an inhabitant of the same state with themselves; they shall name in their ballots the person voted for as President, and in distinct ballots the person voted for as Vice-President, and they shall make distinct lists of all persons voted for as President, and of all persons voted for as Vice-President, and of the number of votes for each, which lists they shall sign and certify, and transmit sealed to the seat of the government of the United States, directed to the President of the Senate;—The President of the Senate shall, in the presence of the Senate and House of Representatives, open all the certificates and the votes shall then be counted;—The person having the greatest number of votes for President, shall be the President, if such number be a majority of the whole number of Electors appointed; and if no person have such majority, then from the persons having the highest numbers not exceeding three on the list of those voted for as President, the House of Representatives shall choose immediately, by ballot, the President. But in choosing the President, the votes shall be taken by states, the representation from each state having one vote; a quorum for this purpose shall consist of a member or members from two-thirds of the states, and a majority of all the states shall be necessary to a choice. And if the House of Representatives shall not choose a President whenever the right of choice shall devolve upon them, before the fourth day of March next following, then the Vice-President shall act as President, as in the case of the death or other constitutional disability of the President.—The person having the greatest number of votes as Vice-President, shall be the Vice-President, if such number be a majority of the whole number of Electors appointed, and if no person have a majority, then from the two highest numbers on the list, the Senate shall choose the Vice-President; a quorum for the purpose shall consist of two-thirds of

the whole number of Senators, and a majority of the whole number shall be necessary to a choice. But no person constitutionally ineligible to the office of President shall be eligible to that of Vice-President of the United States.

ARTICLE XIII
1865

SECTION 1. Neither slavery nor involuntary servitude, except as a punishment for crime whereof the party shall have been duly convicted, shall exist within the United States, or any place subject to their jurisdiction.

SECTION 2. Congress shall have power to enforce this article by appropriate legislation.

ARTICLE XIV
1868

SECTION 1. All persons born or naturalized in the United States, and subject to the jurisdiction thereof, are citizens of the United States and of the State wherein they reside. No State shall make or enforce any law which shall abridge the privileges or immunities of citizens of the United States; nor shall any State deprive any person of life, liberty, or property, without due process of law; nor deny to any person within its jurisdiction the equal protection of the laws.

SECTION 2. Representatives shall be apportioned among the several States according to their respective numbers, counting the whole number of persons in each State, excluding Indians not taxed. But when the right to vote at any election for the choice of electors for President and Vice President of the United States, Representatives in Congress, the

Executive and Judicial officers of a State, or the members of the Legislature thereof, is denied to any of the male inhabitants of such State, being twenty-one years of age, and citizens of the United States, or in any way abridged, except for participation in rebellion, or other crime, the basis of representation therein shall be reduced in the proportion which the number of such male citizens shall bear to the whole number of male citizens twenty-one years of age in such State.

SECTION 3. No person shall be a Senator or Representative in Congress, or elector of President and Vice President, or hold any office, civil or military, under the United States, or under any State, who, having previously taken an oath, as a member of Congress, or as an officer of the United States, or as a member of any State legislature, or as an executive or judicial officer of any State, to support the Constitution of the United States, shall have engaged in insurrection or rebellion against the same, or given aid or comfort to the enemies thereof. But Congress may by a vote of two-thirds of each House, remove such disability.

SECTION 4. The validity of the public debt of the United States, authorized by law, including debts incurred for payment of pensions and bounties for services in suppressing insurrection or rebellion, shall not be questioned. But neither the United States nor any State shall assume or pay any debt or obligation incurred in aid of insurrection or rebellion against the United States, or any claim for the loss or emancipation of any slave; but all such debts, obligations and claims shall be held

illegal and void.

SECTION 5. The Congress shall have power to enforce, by appropriate legislation, the provisions of this article.

ARTICLE XV
1870

SECTION 1. The right of citizens of the United States to vote shall not be denied or abridged by the United States or by any State on account of race, color, or previous condition of servitude—

SECTION 2. The Congress shall have power to enforce this article by appropriate legislation.

ARTICLE XVI
1913

The Congress shall have power to lay and collect taxes on incomes, from whatever source derived, without apportionment among the several States and without regard to any census or enumeration.

ARTICLE XVII
1913

The Senate of the United States shall be composed of two senators from each State, elected by the people thereof, for six years; and each Senator shall have one vote. The electors in each State shall have the qualifications requisite for electors of the most numerous branch of the State legislature.

When vacancies happen in the representation of any State in the Senate, the executive authority of such State shall issue writs of election to fill such vacancies: *Provided,* That the legislature of any State may empower the executive

99

thereof to make temporary appointments until the people fill the vacancies by election as the legislature may direct.

This amendment shall not be so construed as to affect the election of term of any senator chosen before it becomes valid as part of the Constitution.

ARTICLE XVIII
1919

SECTION 1. After one year from the ratification of this article, the manufacture, sale, or transportation of intoxicating liquors within, the importation thereof into, or the exportation thereof from the United States and all territory subject to the jurisdiction thereof for beverage purposes is hereby prohibited.

SECTION 2. The Congress and the several States shall have concurrent power to enforce this article by appropriate legislation.

SECTION 3. This article shall be inoperative unless it shall have been ratified as an amendment to the Constitution by the legislatures of the several States, as provided in the Constitution, within seven years from the date of the submission hereof to the States by Congress.

ARTICLE XIX
1920

The right of citizens of the United States to vote shall not be denied or abridged by the United States or by any States on account of sex.

The Congress shall have power by appropriate legislation to enforce the provisions of this article.

ARTICLE XX
1933

SECTION 1. The terms of the President and Vice-President shall end at noon on the twentieth day of January, and the terms of Senators and Representatives at noon on the third day of January, of the years in which such terms would have ended if this article had not been ratified; and the terms of their successors shall then begin.

SECTION 2. The Congress shall assemble at least once in every year, and such meeting shall begin at noon on the third day of January, unless they shall by law appoint a different day.

SECTION 3. If, at the time fixed for the beginning of the term of the President, the President-elect shall have died, the Vice-President-elect shall become President. If a President shall not have been chosen before the time fixed for the beginning of his term, or if the President-elect shall have failed to qualify, then the Vice-President-elect shall act as President until a President shall have qualified; and the Congress may by law provide for the case wherein neither a President-elect nor a Vice-President-elect shall have qualified, declaring who shall then act as President, or the manner in which one who is to act shall be selected, and such person shall act accordingly until a President or Vice-President shall have qualified.

SECTION 4. The Congress may by law provide for the case of the death of any of the persons from whom the House of Representatives may choose a President whenever the right of choice shall have devolved upon them, and for the case of the death of any of the persons from whom the Senate may choose a Vice-President whenever the right of choice shall have devolved upon them.

SECTION 5. Sections 1 and 2 shall take effect on the 15th day of October following the ratification of this article.

SECTION 6. This article shall be inoperative unless it shall have been ratified as an amendment to the Constitution by the legislatures of three-fourths of the several States within seven years from the date of its submission.

ARTICLE XXI
1933

SECTION 1. The eighteenth article of amendment to the Constitution of the United States is hereby repealed.

SECTION 2. The transportation or importation into any State, Territory, or possession of the United States for delivery or use therein of intoxicating liquors, in violation of the laws thereof, is hereby prohibited.

SECTION 3. This article shall be inoperative unless it shall have been ratified as an amendment to the Constitution by conventions in the several States, as provided in the Constitution, within seven years from the date of the submission hereof to the States by the Congress.

ARTICLE XXII
1951

SECTION 1. No person shall be elected to the office of the

President more than twice, and no person who has held the office of President, or acted as President for more than two years of a term to which some other person was elected President shall be elected to the office of the President more than once. But this Article shall not apply to any person holding the office of President when this Article was proposed by the Congress, and shall not prevent any person who may be holding the office of President, or acting as President, during the term within which this Article becomes operative from holding the office of President or acting as President during the remainder of such term.

SECTION 2. The Congress shall have the power to enforce this article by appropriate legislation.

ARTICLE XXIII
1961

SECTION 1. The District constituting the seat of Government of the United States shall appoint in such manner as the Congress may direct:
A number of electors of President and Vice-President equal to the whole number of Senators and Representatives in Congress to which the District would be entitled if it were a State, but in no event more than the least populous state; they shall be in addition to those appointed by the states, but they shall be considered, for the purposes of the election of President and Vice-President, to be electors appointed by a state; and they shall meet in the District and perform such duties as provided by the twelfth article of amendment.

SECTION 2. The Congress shall have power to enforce this article by appropriate legislation.

ARTICLE XXIV
1964

SECTION 1. The right of citizens of the United States to vote in any primary or other election for President or Vice-President, for electors for President or Vice-President, or for Senator or Representative in Congress, shall not be denied or abridged by the United States or any state by reason of failure to pay any poll tax or other tax.

SECTION 2. The Congress shall have power to enforce this article by appropriate legislation.

ARTICLE XXV
1967

SECTION 1. In case of the removal of the President from office or his death or resignation, the Vice-President shall become President.

SECTION 2. Whenever there is a vacancy in the office of the Vice-President, the President shall nominate a Vice-President who shall take the office upon confirmation by a majority vote of both houses of Congress.

SECTION 3. Whenever the President transmits to the President pro tempore of the Senate and the Speaker of the House of Representatives his written declaration that he is unable to discharge the powers and duties of his office, and until he transmits to them a written declaration to the contrary, such powers and duties shall be discharged by the Vice-President as Acting President.

SECTION 4. Whenever the Vice-President and a majority of either the principal officers of the executive departments, or of such other body as Congress may by law provide, transmit to the President pro tempore of the Senate and the Speaker of the House of Representatives their written declaration that the President is unable to discharge the powers and duties of his office, the Vice-President shall immediately assume the powers and duties of the office as Acting President.

Thereafter, when the President transmits to the President pro tempore of the Senate and the Speaker of the House of Representatives his written declaration that no inability exists, he shall resume the powers and duties of his office unless the Vice-President and a majority of either the principal officers of the executive department, or of such other body as Congress may be law provide, transmit within four days to the President pro tempore of the Senate and the Speaker of the House of Representatives their written declaration that the President is unable to discharge the powers and duties of his office. Thereupon Congress shall decide the issue, assembling within 48 hours for that purpose if not in session. If the Congress, within 21 days after receipt of the latter written declaration, or, if Congress is not in session, within 21 days after Congress is required to assemble, determines by two-thirds vote of both houses that the President is unable to discharge the powers and duties of his office, the Vice-President shall continue to discharge the same as Acting President; otherwise, the President shall resume the powers and duties of his office.

ARTICLE XXVI
1971

SECTION 1. The right of citizens of the United States, who are eighteen years of age or older, to vote shall not be denied or a-bridged by the United States or by any State on account of age.

SECTION 2. The Congress shall have power to enforce this article by appropriate legislation.

UNITED STATES CONSTITUTION
1787

I. Facts and Concepts

A. Article I

1. The House of Representatives and the Senate are in which branch of government: judicial, executive, or legislative?

   _____

2. What are three qualifications a person must meet to become a representative?

   _____

   _____

   _____

3. According to Section 3, who elects senators? Who elects senators now?

   _____

   _____

4. What are three qualifications a person must meet to become a senator?

   _____

   _____

   _____

5. Look up the word "veto" in a dictionary and write down its definition. What section of Article I discusses vetos?

   _____

   _____

6. List five of the powers and duties of Congress.

   _____

   _____

   _____

   _____

B. Article II

7. The president is in which branch of government: executive,
    judicial, or legislative?

    _____

8. What are the three qualifications a person must meet in
    order to be president?

    _____

    _____

    _____

9. List two executive checks over the legislative branch.

    _____

    _____

10. List two executive checks over the judicial branch.

    _____

    _____

11. List three of the powers and duties of the president.

    _____

    _____

    _____

    _____

12. Read Section 1 and answer the following questions.

    a. How are presidential electors selected?

    _____

    _____

    b. Who elects the president if no candidate receives a
       majority in the electoral college vote?

    _____

c. Who takes over the office of president if the president dies or is otherwise removed from office?

_____

d. What body determines the order of succession to the presidency in the event that both the president and the vice-president die or are removed from office?

_____

C. Article III

13. The Supreme Court is in which branch of government: executive, judicial, or legislative?

_____

14. In what types of cases does the Supreme Court have original jurisdiction?

_____

_____

15. Who is allowed to establish courts inferior to the Supreme Court?

_____

16. What check does the second paragraph of Section 2 give Congress over the Supreme Court?

_____

_____

_____

17. State in your own words the main guarantee of the last paragraph of Section 2.

_____

_____

D. Articles IV-VII

18. Explain the main idea of Article IV, Section 1, in your own words.

    _____

    _____

    _____

    _____

19. Look up the word "extradition" in a dictionary and write down its definition. In what article and section is extradition discussed?

    _____

    _____

20. What does the first paragraph of Article IV, Section 3 forbid?

    _____

    _____

21. In your own words, describe the three main statements of Article IV, Section 4.

    _____

    _____

    _____

    _____

22. Read Article V and answer the following questions.

    a. In what two ways can amendments to the Constitution be proposed?

    _____

    _____

b. In what two ways can amendments to the Constitution be ratified?

_____

_____

c. What is each state guaranteed in this article?

_____

_____

23. Read Article VI and answer the following questions.

a. What does this article require of all elected officials in the U.S.?

_____

_____

b. What does this article say can never be used as a requirement for public office in the U.S.?

_____

_____

24. According to Article VII, how many states were required to ratify the Constitution for it to go into effect?

_____

E. The Bill of Rights

25. Look up "eminent domain" and write down its definition. Which of the amendments discusses eminent domain?

_____

_____

26. A list of the ideas in the Bill of Rights appears below. In the space in front of each idea, write the number of the amendment (1 through 10) in which it is found. Amendments will be used more than once in your answers.

_____ a. freedom of speech

_____ b. the states keep all powers not given to the federal government

_____ c. right to a speedy and public trial

_____ d. cruel and unusual punishments are illegal

_____ e. freedom of religion

_____ f. indictment by grand jury before trial

_____ g. right to assemble peacefully

_____ h. freedom from search and seizure except by warrant

_____ i. right to trial by jury in criminal cases

_____ j. right to bear arms

_____ k. freedom of the press

_____ l. trying someone for the same crime twice is illegal

_____ m. accused persons have the right to be informed of the charges against them

_____ n. no quartering of troops in civilian homes

_____ o. right to petition the government

_____ p. a person cannot be forced to testify against himself or herself

_____ q. a person has the right to be confronted with the witnesses against him or her in a trial

_____ r. a person can compel witnesses to appear in his or her favor

_____ s. a person cannot be deprived of life, liberty, or property without due process of law

_____ t. rights enjoyed by U.S. citizens cannot be taken away on the grounds that they do not appear in the Constitution

_____ u. the government cannot take private property for public use unless it pays the owner for the property

_____ v. right to trial by jury in civil cases

_____ w. no excessive bails or fines can be imposed

F. Other Amendments

27. Look up the phrases "poll tax" and "lame duck" and write down their meanings. In which amendments do each of these concepts appear?

_____

_____

_____

_____

_____

28. A list of the ideas in amendments 11 through 26 appears below. In the space in front of each idea, write the number of the amendment in which it is found. Amendments will be used more than once in your answers.

_____ a. slavery abolished

_____ b. federal income tax started

_____ c. alcoholic beverages prohibited

_____ d. separate voting for president and vice-president in the electoral college

_____ e. presidents can only be elected for two terms

_____ f. judicial power of the U.S. does not cover suits brought by the citizens of one state against another state

_____ g. former slaves granted right to vote

_____ h. District of Columbia granted presidential electors

_____ i. eighteen-year-olds granted the right to vote

_____ j. former slaves made citizens of the U.S.

_____ k. former slaves counted as one whole person for purposes of representation in the House

_____ l. officers of the U.S. who rebelled against the government no longer allowed to hold office

_____ m. direct election of senators

_____ n. women granted the right to vote

_____ o. congressional sessions begin January 3 of each year

_____ p. Prohibition repealed

_____ q. neither the U.S. government nor the government of any state will pay debts incurred during a rebellion against the United States

_____ r. poll taxes cannot be used to prevent people from voting in federal elections

_____ s. the vice-president becomes acting president when the president is ill

_____ t. inauguration of the president is January 20

II. For Further Understanding

29. Representation in the House was originally based on the ratio of one representative for every 30,000 people. But as the population grew, it became clear that following this ratio would make governing difficult or impossible. At what number of representatives was the growth of the House stopped? What is the word for the process of redetermining how many representatives each state gets?

_____

_____

30. Who is the only elected officer in the federal government who has duties in two branches of government? (Hint: See Article I, Section 3.) What two branches does he or she serve in?

_____

_____

31. Who originally chose the list of major-party candidates that the electoral college voted on for president and vice-president? Who chooses these candidates now?

_____

_____

32. Who was the only president ever impeached by the House of Representatives? Was he convicted by the Senate?

_____

_____

33. Look up the *Marbury v. Madison* case of 1803 in a history book. After reading about the case, explain what judicial review is. Why is this case important?

_____

_____

_____

_____

_____

34. A part of Article V that is now obsolete says that "no Amendment may be made prior to the Year One thousand eight hundred and eight shall in any Manner affect the first and fourth Clauses in the Ninth Section of the First Article . . . " What geographical section of the country had its interests protected by these clauses from Article I? Explain your answer.

_____

_____

_____

_____

35. The Equal Rights Amendment (ERA) was introduced in Congress in 1923, but never became part of the Constitution. In the space below, write a brief history of the ERA.

_____

_____

_____

_____

_____

_____

_____

36. A famous English document established the basis for the ideas of trial by jury, writs of habeas corpus, and due process of law that appear in the Bill of Rights. What was the name of this document?

_____

37. The Supreme Court has decided many different cases concerning the First Amendment's guarantee of freedom of religion. Choose one of these cases and summarize it below, explaining how the Supreme Court interpreted the First Amendment.

_____

_____

_____

_____

_____

38. What presidential election showed that Amendment 12 was necessary? (Hint: The date of Amendment 12 will help you answer this question.) Explain what happened in this election.

_____

_____

_____

_____

_____

39. Amendment 25, Section 4, establishes the rules for running the national government when the president is incapacitated. Find out about two presidents to whom this amendment would have applied had it existed when they were in office. Briefly describe the situation each president encountered.

_____

_____

_____

_____

_____

_____

_____

KENTUCKY AND VIRGINIA RESOLUTIONS

1798

The Kentucky and Virginia Resolutions are an early example of the process of interpreting and clarifying the Constitution. They forcefully assert the states' rights principle that would be hotly debated throughout early American history and not resolved until the Civil War.

Kentucky Resolutions
November 16, 1798

I. *Resolved,* that the several States composing the United States of America, are not united on the principle of unlimited submission to their general government; but that by compact under the style and title of a Constitution for the United States and of amendments thereto, they constituted a general government for special purposes, delegated to that government certain definite powers, reserving each State to itself, the residuary mass of right to their own self-government; and that whensoever the general government assumes undelegated powers, its acts are unauthoritative, void, and of no force: That to this compact each State acceded as a State, and is an integral party, its co-States forming, as to itself, the other party: That the government created by this compact was not made the exclusive or final judge of the extent of the powers delegated to itself; since that would have made its discretion, and not the Constitution, the measure of its powers; but that as in all other cases of compact among parties having no common Judge, *each party has an equal right to judge for itself, as well of infractions as of the mode and measure of redress.*

II. *Resolved,* that the Constitution of the United States having delegated to Congress a power to punish treason, counterfeiting the securities and current coin of the United States, piracies and felonies committed on the high seas, and offenses against the laws of nations, and no other crimes whatever, and it being true as a general principle, and one of the amendments to the Constitution having also declared "that the powers not delegated to the United States by the Constitution, nor prohibited by it to the States, are reserved to the States respectively, or to the people," therefore also [the Sedition Act of July 14, 1798]; as also the act passed by them on the 27th day of June, 1798, entitled "An act to punish frauds committed on the Bank of the United States" (and all other their acts which assume to create, define, or punish crimes other than those enumerated in the Constitution), are altogether void and of no force, and that the power to create, define, and punish such other crimes is reserved, and of right appertains solely and exclusively to the respective States, each within its own Territory.

III. *Resolved,* that it is true as a general principle, and is also expressly declared by one of the amendments to the Constitution that "the powers not delegated to the United States by the Constitution, nor prohibited by it to the States, are reserved to the States respectively or to the people;" and that no power over the freedom of religion, freedom of speech, or freedom of the press being delegated to the United States by the Constitution, nor prohibited by it to the States, all lawful powers respecting the same did of right remain, and were reserved to the States, or to the people: That thus was manifested their determination to retain to themselves the right of judging how far the licentiousness of speech and of the press may be abridged without lessening their useful freedom, and how far those abuses which cannot be separated from their use should be tolerated rather than the use be destroyed; and thus also they guarded against all abridgment by the United States of the freedom of religious opinions and exercises, and retained to themselves the right of protecting the same, as this State, by a law passed on the general demand of its citizens, had already protected them from all human restraint or interference: And that in addition to this general principle and express declaration, another and more special provision has been made by one of the amendments to the Constitution which expressly declares, that "Congress shall make no law respecting an establishment of religion, or prohibiting the free exercise thereof, or abridging the freedom of speech, or of the press," thereby guarding in the same sentence, and under the same words, the freedom of religion, of speech, and of the press, insomuch, that whatever violates either, throws down the sanctuary which covers the others, and that libels, falsehoods, defamation equally with heresy and false religion, are withheld from the cognizance of Federal tribunals. That therefore [the Sedition Act], which does abridge the freedom of the press, is not law, but is altogether void and of no effect.

IV. *Resolved*, that alien friends are under the jurisdiction and protection of the laws of the State wherein they are; that no power over them has been delegated to the United States, nor prohibited to the individual States distinct from their power over citizens; and it being true as a general principle,

and one of the amendments to the Constitution having also declared that "the powers not delegated to the United States by the Constitution, nor prohibited by it to the States, are reserved to the States respectively, or to the people," the [Alien Act of June 22, 1798], which assumes power over alien friends not delegated by the Constitution, is not law, but is altogether void and of no force.

V. *Resolved*, that in addition to the general principle as well as the express declaration, that powers not delegated are reserved, another and more special provision inserted in the Constitution from abundant caution has declared, "that the migration or importation of such persons as any of the States now existing shall think proper to admit, shall not be prohibited by the Congress prior to the year 1808." That this Commonwealth does admit the migration of alien friends described as the subject of the said act concerning aliens; that a provision against prohibiting their migration is a provision against all acts equivalent thereto, or it would be nugatory; that to remove them when migrated is equivalent to a prohibition of their migration, and is therefore contrary to the said provision of the Constitution, and void.

VI. *Resolved*, that the imprisonment of a person under the protection of the laws of this Commonwealth on his failure to obey the simple order of the President to depart out of the United States, as is undertaken by the said act entitled "An act concerning aliens," is contrary to the Constitution, one amendment to which has provided, that "no person shall be deprived of liberty without due process of law," and that another having provided

116

"that in all criminal prosecutions, the accused shall enjoy the right to a public trial by an impartial jury, to be informed of the nature and cause of the accusation, to be confronted with the witnesses against him, to have compulsory process for obtaining witnesses in his favour, and to have the assistance of counsel for his defense," the same act undertaking to authorize the President to remove a person out of the United States who is under the protection of the law, on his own suspicion, without accusation, without jury, without public trial, without confrontation of the witnesses against him, without having witnesses in his favour, without defense, without counsel, is contrary to these provisions also of the Constitution, is therefore not law, but utterly void and of no force. That transferring the power of judging any person who is under the protection of the laws, from the courts to the President of the United States, as is undertaken by the same act concerning aliens, is against the article of the Constitution which provides, that "the judicial power of the United States shall be vested in courts, the judges of which shall hold their offices during good behavior," and that the said act is void for that reason also; and it is further to be noted, that this transfer of judiciary power is to that magistrate of the general government who already possesses all the executive, and a qualified negative in all the legislative powers.

VII. *Resolved*, that the construction applied by the general government (as is evinced by sundry of their proceedings) to those parts of the Constitution of the United States which delegate to Congress a power to lay and collect taxes, duties, imposts, and excises; to pay the debts, and provide for the common defense, and general welfare of the United States, and to make all laws which shall be necessary and proper for carrying into execution the powers vested by the Constitution in the government of the United States, or any department thereof, goes to the destruction of all the limits prescribed to their power by the Constitution: That words meant by that instrument to be subsidiary only to the execution of the limited powers ought not to be so construed as themselves to give unlimited powers, nor a part so to be taken as to destroy the whole residue of the instrument: That the proceedings of the general government under color of these articles will be a fit and necessary subject for revisal and correction at a time of greater tranquillity, while those specified in the preceding resolutions call for immediate redress.

VIII. *Resolved*, that the preceding Resolutions be transmitted to the Senators and Representatives in Congress from this Commonwealth, who are hereby enjoined to present the same to their respective Houses, and to use their best endeavors to procure, at the next session of Congress, a repeal of the aforesaid unconstitutional and obnoxious acts.

IX. *Resolved*, lastly, that the Governor of this Commonwealth be, and is hereby authorized and requested to communicate the preceding Resolutions to the Legislatures of the several States, to assure them that this Commonwealth considers Union for specified National purposes, and particularly for those specified in their late Federal Compact, to be friendly to the peace, happiness, and prosperity of all the States: that faithful to that compact according to the plain intent and meaning in which it was understood and acceded to by the several parties, it is sincerely anxious for its preservation: that it does also believe, that to take from the States all the powers of self-government, and transfer them to a general and consolidated government, without regard to the special delegations and reservations solemnly agreed to in that compact, is not for the peace, happiness, or prosperity of these States: And that, therefore, this Commonwealth is determined, as it doubts not its co-States are, tamely to submit to undelegated and consequently unlimited powers in no man or body of men on earth: that if the acts before specified should stand, these conclusions would flow from them; that the general government may place any act they think proper on the list of crimes and punish it themselves, whether enumerated or not enumerated by the Constitution as cognizable by them: that they may transfer its cognizance to the President or any other person, who may himself be the accuser, counsel, judge, and jury, whose suspicions may be the evidence, his order the sentence, his officer the executioner, and his breast the sole record of the transaction: that a very numerous and valuable description of the inhabitants of these States being by this precedent reduced as outlaws to the absolute dominion of one man, and the barrier of the Constitution thus swept away from us all, no rampart now remains against the passions and the powers of a majority of Congress, to protect from a like exportation or other more grievous punishment the minority of the same

body, the legislatures, judges, governors, and counselors of the States, nor their other peaceable inhabitants who may venture to reclaim the constitutional rights and liberties of the State and people, or who for other causes, good or bad, may be obnoxious to the views or marked by the suspicions of the President, or be thought dangerous to his or their elections or other interests, public or personal: that the friendless alien has indeed been selected as the safest subject of a first experiment, but the citizen will soon follow, or rather has already followed: for, already has a sedition act marked him as its prey: that these and successive acts of the same character, unless arrested on the threshold, may tend to drive these States into revolution and blood, and will furnish new calumnies against Republican governments, and new pretexts for those who wish it to be believed, that man cannot be governed but by a rod of iron: that it would be a dangerous delusion were a confidence in the men of our choice to silence our fears for the safety of our rights: that confidence is everywhere the parent of despotism: free government is founded in jealousy and not in confidence; it is jealousy and not confidence which prescribes limited Constitutions to bind down those whom we are obliged to trust with power: that our Constitution has accordingly fixed the limits to which and no further our confidence may go; and let the honest advocate of confidence read the alien and sedition acts, and say if the Constitution has not been wise in fixing limits to the government it created, and whether we should be wise in destroying those limits; let him say what the government is if it be not a tyranny, which the men of our choice have conferred on the President, and the President of our choice has assented to and accepted over the friendly strangers, to whom the mild spirit of our country and its laws had pledged hospitality and protection: that the men of our choice have more respected the bare suspicions of the President than the solid rights of innocence, the claims of justification, the sacred force of truth, and the forms and substance of law and justice. In questions of power then let no more be heard of confidence in man, but bind him down from mischief by the claims of the Constitution. That this Commonwealth does therefore call on its co-States for an expression of their sentiments on the acts concerning aliens, and for the punishment of certain crimes herein before specified, plainly declaring whether these acts are or are not authorized by the Federal Compact. And it doubts not that their sense will be so announced as to prove their attachment unaltered to limited government, whether general or particular, and that the rights and liberties of their co-States will be exposed to no dangers by remaining embarked on a common bottom with their own: That they will concur with this Commonwealth in considering the said acts so palpably against the Constitution as to amount to an undisguised declaration, that the compact is not meant to be the measure of the powers of the general government, but that it will proceed in the exercise over these States of all powers whatsoever: That they will view this as seizing the rights of the States and consolidating them in the hands of the general government with a power assumed to bind the

States (not merely in cases made Federal) but in all cases whatsoever, by laws made, not with their consent, but by others against their consent: That this would be to surrender the form of government we have chosen, and to live under one deriving its powers from its own will, and not from our authority; and that the co-States, recurring to their natural right in cases not made Federal, will concur in declaring these acts void and of no force, and will each unite with this Commonwealth in requesting their repeal at the next session of Congress.

Virginia Resolutions
December 24, 1798

Resolved, That the General Assembly of Virginia doth unequivocally express a firm resolution to maintain and defend the Constitution of the United States, and the Constitution of this state, against every aggression either foreign or domestic; and that they will support the Government of the United States in all measures warranted by the former.

That this Assembly most solemnly declares a warm attachment to the union of the states, to maintain which it pledges all its powers; and that, for this end, it is their duty to watch over and oppose every infraction of those principles which constitute the only basis of that Union, because a faithful observance of them can alone secure its existence and the public happiness.

That this Assembly doth explicitly and peremptorily declare that it views the powers of the Federal Government as resulting from the compact to which the states are parties, as limited by the plain sense and intention of the instrument constituting that compact; as no further valid than they are authorized by the grants enumerated in that compact; and that, in case of a deliberate, palpable, and dangerous exercise of other powers not granted by the said compact, the states, who are parties thereto, have the right and are in duty bound to interpose for arresting the progress of the evil, and for maintaining within their respective limits the authorities, rights, and liberties appertaining to them.

That the General Assembly doth also express its deep regret, that a spirit has in sundry instances been manifested by the Federal Government to enlarge its powers by forced constructions of the constitutional charter which defines them; and that indications have appeared of a design to expound certain general phrases (which, having been copied from the very limited grant of powers in the former Articles of Confederation, were the less liable to be misconstrued) so as to destroy the meaning and effect of the particular enumeration which necessarily explains and limits the general phrases; and so as to consolidate the states, by degrees, into one sovereignty, the obvious tendency and inevitable consequence of which would be to transform the present republican system of the United States into an absolute, or, at best, a mixed monarchy.

That the General Assembly doth particularly PROTEST against the palpable and alarming infractions of the Constitution in the two late cases of the "Alien and Sedition Acts," passed at the last session of Congress; the first of which exercises a power nowhere delegated to the Federal Government, and which, by

uniting legislative and judicial powers to those of [the] executive, subverts the general principles of free government, as well as the particular organization and positive provisions of the Federal Constitution: and the other of which acts exercises, in like manner, a power not delegated by the Constitution, but, on the contrary, expressly and positively forbidden by one of the amendments thereto,—a power which, more than any other, ought to produce universal alarm, because it is levelled against the right of freely examining public characters and measures, and of free communication among the people thereon, which has ever been justly deemed the only effectual guardian of every other right.

That this state having, by its Convention which ratified the Federal Constitution, expressly declared that, among other essential rights, "the liberty of conscience and of the press cannot be cancelled, abridged, restrained or modified by any authority of the United States," and from its extreme anxiety to guard these rights from every possible attack of sophistry or ambition, having, with other states, recommended an amendment for that purpose, which amendment was in due time annexed to the Constitution,—it would mark a reproachful inconsistency and criminal degeneracy, if an indifference were now shown to the palpable violation of one of the rights thus declared and secured, and to the establishment of a precedent which may be fatal to the other.

That the good people of this commonwealth, having ever felt and continuing to feel the most sincere affection for their brethren of the other states, the truest anxiety for establishing and

perpetuating the union of all and
the most scrupulous fidelity to
that Constitution, which is the
pledge of mutual friendship, and
the instrument of mutual happiness, the General Assembly doth
solemnly appeal to the like disposi-
tions of the other states, in confidence that they will concur with
this Commonwealth in declaring,
as it does hereby declare, that the
acts aforesaid are unconstitutional;
and that the necessary and proper
measures will be taken by each for
co-operating with this state, in
maintaining unimpaired the
authorities, rights, and liberties
reserved to the states respectively,
or to the people . . .

KENTUCKY AND VIRGINIA RESOLUTIONS

1798

I. Facts and Concepts

A. Kentucky Resolutions

1. Look up the words "alien" and "sedition" in a dictionary and write down their definitions.

   _____

   _____

2. The theory of government described in Section I of this document is often called the compact theory of government. Answer the following questions based on Section I to understand this idea of government.

   a. Who are the members of the compact described in this section?

   _____

   b. According to this section, who has all powers not delegated to the federal government?

   _____

   c. Why does this section say that the federal government should not be the judge of the extent of its own powers?

   _____

   _____

   _____

3. Read Section II and answer the following questions.

   a. What types of laws does this section say are "altogether void and of no force"?

   _____

   _____

b. What power does this section say is reserved to the
   states?

_____

_____

_____

4. Read Section III and answer the following questions.

   a. What law is protested in this section?

   _____

   b. What two parts of the Constitution are quoted to protest
      against this law?

   _____

5. What law is protested in Section IV?

   _____

6. What part of the Constitution is used in Section V to argue
   that the deportation of aliens is unconstitutional?

   _____

7. In your own words, summarize the three arguments made
   in Section VI to show that the imprisonment or deportation
   of aliens is unconstitutional.

   _____

   _____

   _____

   _____

   _____

   _____

   _____

8. Look up the phrases "strict construction" and "loose construction" of the Constitution in a history or government book and explain their meanings. Which of the two ideas does Section VII support?

_____

_____

_____

_____

_____

9. Read Section IX and answer the following questions.

a. What do the authors of this document pledge their support to in the early part of this section?

_____

b. Explain in your own words the meaning of the following phrase: "it would be a dangerous delusion were a confidence in the men of our choice to silence our fears for the safety of our rights . . . "

_____

_____

_____

c. What does this section call on the other states to do?

_____

_____

B. Virginia Resolutions

10. According to the first two paragraphs of this document, does Virginia support or oppose the union and the federal government? Does it support or oppose the Constitution?

_____

_____

11. Read the paragraph that begins, "That this Assembly doth . . . " and answer the following questions.

a. According to this paragraph, what is the source of the power of the federal government?

_____

b. This paragraph says that the powers of the federal government are limited by "the instrument constituting that compact, ... " What is this "instrument"?

_____

c. Who has the power to stop the federal government from a "deliberate, palpable, and dangerous exercise of other powers ... "?

_____

_____

12. In the paragraph that begins, *That the General Assembly doth particularly* ... what two acts are protested?

_____

13. What does the last paragraph of this document call on the other states to do?

_____

_____

C. Comparison of the Kentucky and Virginia Resolutions

14. Give a quotation from each document showing that each supports the compact theory of government.

_____

_____

_____

_____

_____

_____

_____

15. According to both documents, what is the instrument that keeps the federal government in check?

_____

16. According to both documents, who has the power to decide whether or not a law is constitutional?

_____

II. For Further Understanding

17. Who wrote the Kentucky Resolutions? Who wrote the Virginia Resolutions?

_____

_____

18. Look up the two acts protested by these resolutions and state briefly the provisions of each.

_____

_____

_____

_____

_____

_____

_____

19. What finally happened to the acts that these resolutions protested?

_____

_____

_____

20. Look up the theory of states' rights and explain what it means. Which section of the country was most in favor of the idea of states' rights?

_____

_____

_____

_____

ANSWER KEY

Albany Plan of Union

1. The purpose of this document is to outline a plan for "one general government" for the American colonies.

2. The introductory paragraph says that under the new plan "each colony may retain its present constitution . . ."

3. a. The president-general is to be appointed by the king or queen of England.

   b. The assemblies of each of the colonies will send representatives to the Grand Council.

4. three years

5. a. After the first three years the government is in effect, the number of representatives each colony sends to the Grand Council will be determined by the proportion of money each contributes to the general treasury.

   b. answers will vary

6. a. The Grand Council is supposed to meet in regular session once a year.

   b. The president-general has the power to call an emergency meeting of the Grand Council.

7. a. To prorogue is to discontinue a session of an assembly.

   b. The Grand Council cannot be dissolved, prorogued, or held in session for longer than six weeks at a time without its consent or by a special command of the king or queen.

8. a. This phrase means that the president-general has the power to veto legislation passed by the Grand Council.

   b. The main duty of the president-general is to execute the laws.

9. Sections 10, 11, and 12 give the Grand Council the power to do the following five things with regard to Indians: make treaties, declare war, make peace, regulate trade, and purchase lands.

10. a. The Grand Council is allowed to create and support an army and a navy.

    b. To impress is to force a person to serve in the military.

11. Section 16 gives the Grand Council the power to make laws and levy taxes.

12. The phrase "each government" refers to the internal government of each of the colonies.

13. a. A quorum is the minimum number of members of a legislative body who must be present to do business.

   b. Twenty-five members constitutes a quorum in the Grand Council.

14. a. The laws of the colonial government must agree with the laws of England.

   b. The king or queen of England has the final power to approve or disapprove laws passed by the Grand Council.

15. Under this plan, the three-step process by which a bill would become a law is as follows: the bill would be passed by the Grand Council, approved by the president-general, and approved by the king or queen of England.

16. Benjamin Franklin

17. In 1754 the colonies were on the verge of becoming involved in the French and Indian War. The representatives met at Albany to try to win the support of the Iroquois Indians, and realized that they needed unity to be able to negotiate with the Indians.

18. The Albany Plan was never adopted, because neither the colonies nor the British government approved of it. The colonies did not want to give up any of their powers to a central government, and the British did not want the colonies to have the degree of control over their own affairs that a central government would give them.

19. The judicial branch is not included in the Albany Plan.

20. 1. the vice-president
    2. the speaker of the House of Representatives
    3. the president *pro tempore* of the Senate
    4. the Secretary of State
    5. the Secretary of the Treasury

Declaration and Resolves of the First Continental Congress

1. Any five of the following may be listed: the British had claimed the right to legislate in all matters in the colonies, the British had imposed direct taxes, the British had imposed indirect taxes, the British had created a board of commissioners with unconstitutional powers, the British had extended the jurisdiction of admiralty courts, judges in the colonies were made dependent on the king for their salaries, standing armies had been kept in the colonies during peacetime, and some colonists accused of crimes had been forced to go to England for their trials.

2. In the third paragraph, the colonists protest the passage of four unjust and unconstitutional statutes against the American colonies.

3. The two grievances listed in this paragraph are as follows: colonial assemblies had been repeatedly dissolved, and colonial petitions to the king had been treated with contempt.

4. To protect their rights, the colonists had elected deputies to sit in a general congress.

5. The three sources of rights that the colonists list are: the laws of nature, the English constitution, and the charters or compacts of the individual colonies.

6. In these sections, the colonists claim the right to life, liberty, and property; that their ancestors were entitled to full rights as English citizens at the time they emigrated to the colonies; and that their ancestors did not forfeit these rights, but kept them and passed them on to their descendants.

7. a. The basic right outlined in this section is the right of people to participate in their own government.

   b. According to this section, the colonists are not represented in the British Parliament.

   c. Since the colonists cannot be represented in Parliament, they claim the right to have "free and exclusive power of legislation" in their colonial assemblies.

   d. The king would have the right to veto colonial laws.

   e. The colonists were willing to honor laws to regulate external trade to the commercial advantage of England.

   f. The colonists denied that Parliament had the right to pass laws of taxation without the consent of the colonists.

8. In these sections the colonists claimed the right to follow the common law of England, the right to be tried by their peers, the benefit of established laws at the time of colonization; all privileges granted by royal charters or provincial laws, the right to peaceably assemble; and the right to petition the king.

9. a. The separation of the branches of government is described as necessary to good government in this section.

   b. The colonists claimed that the king had violated this condition by creating a legislative councils in several colonies.

10. a. The colonists "claim, demand, and insist on" all the rights and liberties previously mentioned in the document.

    b. These rights may only be taken from the colonists with their consent.

11. This paragraph resolves that the acts of Parliament to be listed next must be repealed in order to restore good relations between Great Britain and the colonies.

12. The colonists found the following violations of their rights in the laws named in this paragraph: extending the powers of the admiralty courts beyond their ancient limits, depriving Americans of trial by jury, protecting the prosecutor in a trial from damages for which he might ordinarily be liable, and demanding excessive payment from people claiming ships and goods that have been seized.

13. a. A vicinage is the region around a particular area.

    b. The colonists contended that they were being denied the right of trial by a jury of people from the area around where a crime was committed.

14. The colonists protest the act for stopping the port and blocking the harbor of Boston, the act for altering the charter and government of Massachusetts, and the act "for the better administration of Justice."

15. a. The colonists hope that the British will revise the laws.

    b. To protest these laws, the colonists decided to enter into an agreement not to import British goods or export their goods to Britain. They also decided to prepare an address to the British people and an address to the British king.

16. the French and Indian War

17. the Intolerable Acts

18. King George III of England

19. boycott

20. The actions taken by the colonists described in this document were not successful. The British did not change the laws, the colonists became more dissatisfied with British rule, and eventually the revolutionary war broke out.

Common Sense

1. This essay tries to persuade the colonies to declare their independence from Great Britain.

2. a. Paine says that the "period of debate" is closed because the debates have not led to any solutions, and people have turned to arms as a last resort.

   b. the king of England

   c. Paine is referring to the continent of North America.

3. The main idea of the third paragraph is that an entire continent is involved in the struggle and that its outcome will affect all posterity.

4. a. The beginning of hostilities between the two sides on April 19, 1775, caused their relationship to go "from argument to arms."

   b. Before that event, all of the arguments on both sides favored continued union with Great Britain.

   c. Britain proposed force in achieving its ends, and the colonies proposed friendship.

5. a. The following phrase shows that Paine no longer thought that reconciliation was possible: "reconciliation, . . . like an agreeable dream, has passed away and left us as we were, . . . "

   b. Paine said he would investigate the following four things in the next part of his essay: the injuries the colonies would suffer if they remained dependent on Britain, the union of the colonies with Britain in the light of nature and common sense, the aspects of independence, and what the colonists could expect if they remained dependent.

6. a. The first argument that Paine deals with is the argument that America has flourished under British protection.

   b. Paine refutes this argument by saying "America would have flourished as much, and probably much more, had no European power taken any notice of her."

7. Paine argues against the viewpoint that Britain had protected the colonies.

8. a. Paine says Britain protected its American colonies out of self-interest.

b. Paine says that with independence the colonies would be at peace with Spain and France even if Britain was at war with those countries.

9. a. Paine argues against the viewpoint that the colonies should remain united with Britain because Britain is their parent country.

   b. According to Paine, most of the people in the colonies fled from Europe to escape civil and religious persecution.

10. Paine uses this idea to show his belief that the idea that England should rule the colonies because the colonists are of English descent is absurd.

11. a. Paine argues against the viewpoint that a united Britain and colonies could rule the world.

    b. Paine dismisses this argument by saying that Americans would never fight in British wars in Asia, Africa, or Europe.

12. According to this paragraph, commerce will secure America the peace and friendship of all of Europe.

13. In this paragraph, Paine says that there are no advantages to American connection with Britain.

14. The paragraph marked *First* argues that if the colonies declared their independence from Britain, a third country could act as mediator in their conflict. The paragraph marked *Secondly* argues that France and Spain will be unlikely to help the colonies unless they declare their independence. The paragraph marked *Thirdly* argues that by declaring their independence the colonies would cease to be rebels in the eyes of other countries. The paragraph marked *Fourthly* argues that a declaration of independence, including the reasons for independence, directed at European countries, would do more good than petitions to Britain.

15. Paine is referring to the Battle of Lexington and Concord, which took place on April 19, 1775.

16. The Declaration of Independence was issued in July 1776, seven months after the publication of *Common Sense*.

17. Paine also supported the French Revolution. The major work he wrote during that revolution was called *The Rights of Man*.

18. Thomas Paine was born in England in 1737. He went to America in 1774. He quickly became a strong supporter of the independence movement. In 1776 he wrote *Common Sense* and another series of pamphlets called *The Crisis*. After the

American Revolution, Paine supported the French Revolution. He wrote two famous books, *The Rights of Man* and *The Age of Reason*, during the French Revolution and became a French citizen in 1792. He later angered leaders of the revolution, however, and was imprisoned. He returned to America in 1802 and died an outcast in 1809.

Declaration of Independence

1. The following phrase from the first paragraph announces that the colonies are going to declare their independence: "to dissolve the political bands which have connected them with another, and to assume, among the Powers of the earth, the separate and equal station to which the Laws of Nature and of Nature's God entitle them . . ."

2. The first paragraph says that "a decent respect to the opinions of mankind" requires that the colonists must explain why they are declaring independence.

3. Unalienable means not to be separated. The three unalienable rights listed in the document are life, liberty, and the pursuit of happiness.

4. According to this document, governments are instituted to secure the unalienable rights of life, liberty, and the pursuit of happiness.

5. Governments get their power from the consent of the governed.

6. A people have a right to overthrow their government whenever the government becomes destructive of the rights of the people.

7. The author of the Declaration uses the phrase "absolute Tyranny" to describe the British government over the colonies.

8. Answers will vary, because many of the grievances mention legislative bodies.

9. Answers will vary, because many of the grievances mention the legal system.

10. According to three of the grievances, the British had enlisted the following three groups of people to fight against the colonists: foreign mercenaries, other English citizens, and Indians.

11. The document says that the colonists had petitioned the king and the British people to try to get the British to change their policies.

12. In the following phrase, the colonists officially declare their independence: "these united Colonies are, and of Right ought to be, Free and Independent states; . . . they are absolved from all Allegiance to the British Crown, and . . . all political connection between them and the State of Great Britain is, and ought to be, totally dissolved; . . . "

13. The colonies claim to have the power to make war and peace, make alliances, establish commerce, and do all other things that free and independent states do.

14. "He" is King George III of England.

15. Thomas Jefferson

16. Any four of the following may be listed:

    1. *Action:* the port of Boston was closed. *Grievance:* "for cutting off our trade with all parts of the world."
    2. *Action:* the charter of Massachusetts was revoked. *Grievance:* "for taking away our charters, abolishing our most valuable laws, and altering fundamentally, the forms of our governments."
    3. *Action:* the Massachusetts legislature and courts were prohibited from holding sessions. *Grievance:* "for suspending our own legislatures, . . . ," or "he has dissolved representative houses repeatedly, . . . "
    4. *Action:* local government in Massachusetts was placed under military control. *Grievance:* "he has effected to render the military independent of, and superior to, the civil power."
    5. *Action:* town meetings were not allowed to be held. *Grievance:* "he has dissolved representative houses repeatedly . . . " or "for taking away our charters, abolishing our most valuable laws, and altering fundamentally, the forms of our governments."
    6. *Action:* more troops were brought into Massachusetts. *Grievance:* he has kept among us in times of peace, standing armies, without the consent of our legislatures."
    7. *Action:* the Quartering Act was revived in Boston. *Grievance:* "for quartering large bodies of armed troops among us."

17. John Adams and Thomas Jefferson

18. the Continental Congress

19. The American Revolution inspired the leaders of the French Revolution, which broke out in 1789.

The Crisis

1. a. The "summer soldier" and the "sunshine patriot" were people who would support a cause only when things were going well for the cause.

    b. Paine says that freedom has such a high price because it is so valuable.

    c. Paine tried to provoke the anger of the colonists by saying that the British had declared that they had a right to rule over the colonists in all issues, and that such a situation amounted to slavery of the colonists.

2. Paine reveals in this paragraph that he thinks the Declaration of Independence should have been made sooner. He says, "my own simple opinion is, that had it been eight months earlier it would have been much better."

3. a. Paine believes that God is on the side of the colonists because he believes that God could not desert the colonies after they had tried so hard to avoid war.

    b. Paine believes that God would not support the king of England because of all the king has done to the colonies.

4. a. In the battle described here, the colonial army was less than one fourth the size of the British.

    b. General William Howe commanded the British troops at this battle.

    c. American troops were garrisoned at Fort Lee, which was commanded by Major General Nathanael Greene.

    d. General George Washington commanded all American troops.

    e. The American troops were trying to secure a bridge over the Hackensack River and were trying to march troops away from Fort Lee until they could be reinforced by the New Jersey or Pennsylvania militia.

5. In this paragraph, Paine describes the soldiers who marched with Washington as "greatly harassed and fatigued, frequently without rest, covering, or provision . . . "

6. a. Paine urges the colonies to support the revolutionary war in this paragraph.

b. Paine's "own line of reasoning" is that offensive wars are unjust, but that the colonies are fighting a purely defensive war against a king trying to bind them to his absolute will.

c. King George III of England

7. a. Paine uses the following phrase to reassure the colonists about the war: "I see no real cause for fear. I know our situation well, and I can see the way out of it."

b. Paine praises the American army for making an orderly retreat for almost a hundred miles, for carrying their ammunition with them, for keeping most of their supplies away from the British, and for crossing four rivers successfully in their retreat.

8. a. According to Paine, in the next campaign the army will have sixty thousand well-armed and well-clothed soldiers.

b. Paine says that the following "evils" would result from submission to the British: a ravaged country, a depopulated city, unsafe homes, slavery, homes turned into barracks and houses of prostitution for Hessian soldiers, and a future race of children whose fathers are unknown.

9. The revolutionary war started with the battles of Lexington and Concord in 1775. Other battles took place in 1775 outside Boston and in Canada. In 1776 the colonies declared their independence. Later that year the British invaded New York, forcing the colonists under George Washington to retreat across Pennsylvania into New Jersey. This campaign is described by Paine in *The Crisis*. He wanted to renew the initial enthusiasm of the colonists so that they would not lose hope that they could turn back the British advance.

10. Trenton, New Jersey

11. The Declaratory Act of 1766 said that Parliament had the "full power and authority to make laws to bind the colonies and people of America . . . in all cases whatsoever."

12. Philadelphia was the capital of the colonies during the revolutionary war. The British advance through New Jersey into Pennsylvania threatened Philadelphia. The British later temporarily captured Philadelphia, forcing the Continental Congress to move out of the city.

Articles of Confederation

1. The confederacy formed under this document was named the United States of America.

2. Article II guaranteed the states that their right to govern themselves would not be taken away by the confederation.

3. According to Article III, the states organized into a confederation for the following three reasons: for common defense, to secure their liberties, and for their mutual and general welfare.

4. a. The "free inhabitants of each of these states" were entitled to the privileges and immunities of citizens in any of the other states.

   b. To ingress is to enter and to regress is to go out or go back.

   c. The right of "free ingress and regress" described here is the right of a citizen of one state to go into and come out of any other state.

   d. Extradition is the process of returning a prisoner to the place where he or she committed a crime. The second paragraph of this article says "If any Person guilty of, or charged with treason, felony or other high misdemeanor in any state, shall flee from Justice, and be found in any of the united states, he shall upon demand of the Governor or executive power, of the state from which he fled, be delivered up and removed to the state having jurisdiction of his offence."

   e. The third paragraph says that all states must respect the records, acts, and judicial proceedings of the courts and magistrates of the other states.

5. a. The legislature of each state determined the method by which its delegates to Congress were selected.

   b. The power to recall delegates would insure the state's control over its representatives. If the delegates were not responding to the wishes of the people of the state, they could be recalled and replaced.

   c. Each state could send no fewer than two and no more than seven delegates to Congress.

   d. Delegates could serve in Congress for three years out of any six years.

   e. Each state had one vote in Congress.

   f. Members of Congress are guaranteed the right of free speech and debate in Congress and freedom from arrest during the time they travelled to and from Congress in the last paragraph of this article.

6. a. No. Article VI says that "No state without the Consent of the united states in congress assembled, shall send any embassy to, . . . any king, prince, or state . . . "

   b. No. Article VI says that "No state shall lay any imposts or duties, which may interfere with any stipulations in treaties, entered into by the united states in congress assembled, . . . "

   c. No. Article VI says "nor shall the united states in congress assembled, or any of them, grant any title of nobility."

   d. No. Article VI says that "No two or more states shall enter into any treaty, confederation or alliance whatever between them, without the consent of the united states in congress assembled, . . . "

   e. During peacetime, states could keep a force of "such number only, as in the judgment of the united states in congress assembled, shall be deemed requisite to garrison the forts necessary for the defence of such state; . . . "

   f. Yes. Article VI says "No state shall engage in any war without the consent of the united states in congress assembled, unless such state be actually invaded by enemies, . . . "

7. a. The confederation agreed to pay for all expenses of war, and for all charges incurred for the common defense or general welfare.

   b. The amount of tax each state had to pay to the confederation was based on the value of the land in the state.

   c. The states. This article says, "taxes . . . shall be laid and levied by the authority and direction of the legislatures of the several states . . . "

8. a. Article IX, paragraph one, grants the confederacy the following powers: to make war and peace, to send and receive ambassadors, to enter into treaties and alliances, to establish rules for captures on land and sea, to grant letters of marque and reprisal during peacetime, and to appoint courts to try cases of crimes on the high seas.

   b. Congress was the "last resort on appeal" for all disputes arising between states concerning boundary, jurisdiction, or any other cause.

c. Commissioners or judges of the confederacy had to take an oath from one of the judges of the supreme or superior court of the state in which the dispute they were deciding was being tried.

d. In the fourth paragraph, Congress is granted the power to regulate the value of money, fix standards of weights and measures, regulate trade and manage affairs with Indians, establish post offices, appoint all officers in the service of the United States, and make rules for the army and the navy.

e. In the fifth paragraph, Congress is granted the power to appoint a committee of the states to sit when Congress is recessed, to appoint one of their members to be president, to determine the amount of money needed to defray public expenses, to borrow money, to build and equip a navy, to agree upon the number of land forces necessary and to requisition that number from the states.

f. In most cases, a majority of the states had to approve actions of Congress. In some specific instances listed in this paragraph, nine states had to approve.

9. According to Article XI, nine states would have to consent before Florida could be admitted as a state.

10. In Article XII, the confederation pledged to pay all debts contracted by Congress before the formation of the United States.

11. a. The main idea of the first sentence of this article is that all states of the confederation must abide by the decisions of Congress.

b. This article says that the Articles of Confederation cannot be amended without the consent of all of the states.

12. According to the last paragraph, the signers of the Articles guaranteed by their signatures that they ratified each of the articles, that the constituents of their states would abide by the decisions of Congress, that the Articles would be observed by their states, and that the union created by the Articles would be perpetual.

13. The Articles of Confederation did not provide for an executive or a judicial branch.

14. Answers will vary because the framers of the Constitution found many weaknesses in the Articles of Confederation. Following are some examples: the lack of an executive branch and a judicial branch, the fact that Congress could not tax the states or regulate trade among them, the fact that each state was given one vote in Congress regardless of its size or its population, the fact that all of the states had to consent to amendments to the Articles.

15. Maryland refused to ratify the Articles until the question of conflicting claims to western lands was settled. When other states agreed to surrender their western land claims to the confederation, Maryland signed the Articles on March 1, 1781.

16. The Second Continental Congress governed the United States between the date of the Declaration of Independence and the date when the Articles of Confederation went into effect.

Land Ordinance of 1785

1. The two conditions that determined the types of land that came under the jurisdiction of this ordinance were: the land had to be given up by the individual states, and had to be purchased from the Indians.

2. When they joined together under the Articles of Confederation, all of the states had to surrender their claims to western lands to the Confederation. To insure that the division of land would be completed fairly, it was important that the survey team include representatives of each state.

3. Townships created under this document were six square miles in size.

4. To make sure that the survey was accurate, the Geographer of the United States had to personally survey the first east-west line, determine the latitudes of the extreme ends of the first north-south line, and determine the latitudes of the mouths of the principal rivers in the survey.

5. A chap is a split or opening. A plat is a plan or map. Specie is money in the form of coins.

6. Some of the surveyed land was to be reserved for the use of the members of the former Continental army.

7. The minimum price for an acre of land under this ordinance was one dollar.

8. a. Lot number 16 of each township was to be reserved for the maintenance of public schools in the township.

   b. One third of the mining resources of each township was to be reserved for the U.S. government.

9. The Land Ordinance of 1785 was designed for all of the lands between the Appalachian Mountains and the Mississippi River, and especially for the Northwest Territory.

10. The Land Ordinance of 1785 governed the division and sale of western lands until 1862.

11. the Homestead Act of 1862

12. the Articles of Confederation

Virginia Statute of Religious Liberty

1. Temporal means of or relating to earthly life. Hypocrisy is pretending to be what one is not or to believe what one does not. Ecclesiastical means of or relating to a church. Emolument is profit derived from office or employment.

2. According to Section I, God created the human mind free.

3. "Civil incapacitations" means violations of civil rights.

4. According to Section I, attempts to limit the human mind "beget habits of hypocrisy and meanness . . . "

5. This phrase means that God had power over the bodies and minds of people, and could force them to think only in certain ways, but chose not to.

6. According to Section I, the result of this was the establishment of false religions throughout much of the world.

7. Section I says the practice of forcing people to pay for the support of religious opinions they do not believe in is "sinful and tyrannical."

8. Section I says civil rights are no more dependent on religious opinions than they are on opinions about physics or geometry.

9. This phrase means to prevent a person from holding a public office unless he or she vows to support or reject certain religious beliefs.

10. According to Section I, the only time that public officers are justified in interfering with personal principles is when those principles "break out into overt acts against peace and good order, . . . "

11. Section II makes the following four guarantees: that no one can be compelled to support a religion, that no one can be made to suffer because of his or her religious beliefs, that all people will be free to profess their religious opinions, and that religious opinions will not affect civil opportunities.

12. In Section III, the authors of this document say that while they cannot lawfully declare that this law can never be revoked, they believe that to revoke it would be an infringement of natural right.

13. the Anglican Church

14. Thomas Jefferson

15. the First Amendment

16. The Maryland Toleration Act allowed religious freedom only to those who professed a belief in Jesus Christ. This statute allowed religious freedom to all people, regardless of belief.

Northwest Ordinance

1. The area governed by this ordinance was northwest of the Ohio River.

2. The governor of the territory was appointed by Congress. The governor served for a term of three years.

3. The secretary of the territory was appointed by Congress. The secretary was to keep and preserve the laws passed by the legislature, the territory's public records, and the governor's proceedings, and give copies of them to the secretary of Congress every six months.

4. Three judges were appointed to the territory.

5. The governor and the judges were designated to provide laws for the territory until a general assembly could be organized.

6. a. five thousand

   b. five hundred

   c. The legislature began regulating the number and proportion of representatives after the size of the legislature reached twenty-five members.

   d. In order to be elected a representative, a person had to be a citizen of the U.S. for three years and a resident of the district (or a resident of the district for three years), and had to own two hundred acres of land.

e. In order to elect representatives, a person had to be a citizen of one of the states and a resident of the district (or a resident of the district for two years), and had to own fifty acres of land.

7. a. The governor, the legislative council, and the house of representatives made up the legislature.

   b. There were five members on the legislative council, and they served for five years.

   c. The members of the legislative council were chosen in the following manner. The representatives met at a time and place appointed by the governor and nominated ten people for the council. These ten nominations were sent to Congress, which selected five people from the list to serve on the council.

   d. Yes. The paragraph says "all bills, having passed by a majority in the house, and by a majority in the council, shall be referred to the governor for his assent; but no bill or legislative act whatever, shall be of any force without his assent."

   e. To prorogue is to discontinue a session of a legislative body. Besides the right to veto, the governor had the power to call the assembly into session, discontinue a session of the assembly, and dismiss the assembly.

8. a. The territory's representative to Congress was elected by a joint session of the legislative council and the house of representatives.

   b. The representative could participate in debates in Congress, but could not vote.

9. This paragraph provides for "the establishment of States, ... and for their admission to a share in the federal councils on an equal footing with the original States, ... "

10. Article I guarantees freedom of religious worship.

11. Any three of the following may be listed: a guarantee of the writ of habeas corpus, trial by jury, proportional representation in the legislature, judicial proceedings according to common law, bail for all offences except capital crimes, moderate fines, no cruel and unusual punishments, no taking of property without the judgment of peers or by the law of the land, full compensation for property taken for public use, no laws that interfere with private contracts.

12. a. The beginning of this article encourages the establishment of schools, because "Religion, morality, and knowledge, [are] necessary to good government..."

b. This article encourages that "The utmost good faith... be observed towards the Indians;..."

13. a. Not less than three nor more than five states were to be formed out of this territory.

b. The only requirement for statehood listed in this article is that the prospective state have sixty thousand free inhabitants.

c. This article says that the new state governments must be republican.

14. a. No. This article says that "There shall be neither slavery nor involuntary servitude in the said territory,..."

b. The main idea of the second part of this article is that fugitive slaves from slave states can be reclaimed and returned to the states from which they escaped.

15. the Land Ordinance of 1785

16. Ohio, Indiana, Illinois, Michigan, and Wisconsin

17. no

18. According to Article II, Section 3, of the Constitution, the president can convene special sessions of Congress under extraordinary circumstances. He cannot prorogue or dissolve Congress. He can, however, adjourn Congress if both houses cannot agree on a date of adjournment.

The Federalist, no. 10

1. a. Madison says that one of the greatest advantages of a "well-constructed Union" is "its tendency to break and control the violence of faction."

b. The "instability, injustice, and confusion introduced into the public councils" have been the "mortal diseases" of popular governments in the past.

c. The three complaints "everywhere heard" about governments in the United States were that they were too unstable, that the public good was disregarded in conflicts between rival parties, and that decisions were too often made by the pressures of the majority rather than by the rules of justice and the rights of the minority.

2. Madison defines a faction as a group of people, either a minority or a majority of the population, that have a common interest that goes against the general interest of the community.

3. Madison says that the "mischiefs of faction" can be cured by either removing the causes of faction or controlling its effects.

4. Madison says that the causes of faction can be removed by destroying liberty or by giving each citizen the same opinions, passions, and interests. He thinks the first of these is worse than the disease of faction, and that the second is impractical.

5. Madison says that the "most common and durable" source of factions is the unequal distribution of property.

6. In this paragraph, Madison concludes that since the causes of faction cannot be controlled, the only way to deal with it is by controlling its effects.

7. a. By the "republican principle" Madison means the regular process by which an elected government votes on issues.

   b. When a majority is included in a faction, it can sacrifice the public good to its interest.

8. According to this paragraph, the dangers of a majority faction can be prevented by preventing the majority of the people from having the same passion or interest, or by rendering the majority unable to carry their ideas into effect.

9. No. In this paragraph Madison says that "a pure democracy . . . can admit of no cure for the mischiefs of faction."

10. Madison defines a republic in this paragraph as "a government in which the scheme of representation takes place."

11. Madison says that the two main differences between a democracy and a republic are that government is delegated in a republic, and a republic can be used to govern a large number of citizens in a large area.

12. One advantage of a republic over a democracy is that the dangers of faction are greatly lessened in a republic.

13. The main idea of this paragraph is that large republics have the same advantage over small republics that small republics have over democracies, and that the United States has this advantage over the individual states.

14. The basic idea of this document is that one of the most important functions of government is to control factions, and that a large republic, such as the United States, is the best way to accomplish this goal.

15. the Articles of Confederation

16. The two groups that debated whether or not the Constitution should be ratified were called the Federalists and the Anti-Federalists. The main issue they differed on was the amount of power that the federal government should have.

17. Answers will vary because of the many special-interest groups in the U.S. today.

United States Constitution

1. The House of Representatives and the Senate are in the legislative branch.

2. To become a representative, a person must be at least twenty-five years old, must be a citizen of the United States for at least seven years, and must be an inhabitant of the state he or she is elected from.

3. According to Section 3, senators are elected by the legislatures of the states. Now, senators are elected by the people of the states.

4. To become a senator, a person must be at least thirty years old, must be a citizen of the United States for at least nine years, and must be an inhabitant of the state he or she is elected from.

5. To veto is to reject a bill that has been passed by a legislative body. Section 7 discusses vetos.

6. Any five of the items in Section 8 may be listed.

7. The president is in the executive branch.

8. To be president, a person must be a natural-born citizen of the United States (or a citizen at the time of the adoption of the Constitution), must be thirty-five years old, and must have been a resident of the United States for fourteen years.

9. Any two of the following may be listed: the president can veto legislation, negotiate treaties, and appoint officers of the United States.

10. Two executive checks over the judicial branch are: the president can appoint Supreme Court justices and other federal judges and can grant reprieves and pardons for offenses against the United States.

11. Any three of the items in Sections 2 and 3 may be listed.

12. a. Each state directs the way that its electors will be selected.

    b. The House of Representatives determines who becomes president if no candidate receives a majority in the electoral college vote.

    c. The vice-president takes over the office of president if the president dies or is otherwise removed from office.

    d. Congress determines the order of succession to the presidency in the event that both the president and the vice-president die or are removed from office.

13. The Supreme Court is in the judicial branch.

14. The Supreme Court has original jurisdiction in all cases affecting ambassadors, other public ministers and consuls, and those in which a state is a party.

15. Congress is allowed to establish courts inferior to the Supreme Court.

16. This paragraph gives Congress the power to make exceptions and regulations to the rule that the Supreme Court will have appellate jurisdiction in all the types of cases previously mentioned in this article.

17. The main guarantee of the last paragraph of Section 2 is that the trial of all crimes will be by jury, except in cases of impeachment.

18. Article IV, Section 1, says that each state must recognize the laws, records, and trial results of the other states.

19. Extradition is the process of returning a prisoner to the place in which he or she committed a crime. It is discussed in Article IV, Section 2.

20. This paragraph forbids forming states within the jurisdiction of other states, or combining states without the consent of the legislatures of the states concerned.

21. The three main statements of Article IV, Section 4, are that the United States will guarantee every state a republican form of government, that the federal government will protect the states against invasion, and (when the legislature or executive of a state asks) will protect them against domestic violence.

22. a. Amendments can be proposed by Congress or by a convention called for that purpose.

b. Amendments can be ratified by state legislatures or conventions in three-fourths of the states.

c. In Article V each state is guaranteed that it will not be deprived of equal representation in the Senate without its consent.

23. a. This article requires all elected officials to take an oath or affirmation to uphold the Constitution.

b. This article says that a religious test can never be used as a requirement for public office in the U.S.

24. According to Article VII, nine states were required to ratify the Constitution for it to go into effect.

25. Eminent domain is the right of government to take private property if it is needed for public use. Amendment V discusses eminent domain.

26. a. 1; b. 10; c. 6; d. 8; e. 1; f. 5; g. 1; h. 4; i. 6; j. 2; k. 1; l. 5; m. 6; n. 3; o. 1; p. 5; q. 6; r. 6; s. 5; t. 9; u. 5; v. 7; w. 8.

27. A poll tax is a tax that all people, regardless of their income or property, must pay equally. Poll taxes have often been used by states as a requirement for voting. Amendment 24 says that the right of citizens to vote cannot be denied because of failure to pay a poll tax. A lame duck is a public official who has been defeated for reelection and is serving out the last part of his or her term. Amendment 20, often called the "lame duck amendment," moves the date at which the president and members of Congress leave office closer to election day.

28. a. 13; b. 16; c. 18; d. 12; e. 22; f. 11; g. 15; h. 23; i. 26; j. 14; k. 14; l. 14; m. 17; n. 19; o. 20; p. 21; q. 14; r. 24; s. 25; t. 20.

29. The growth of the House was stopped at 435 representatives. The process of redetermining how many representatives each state gets is called reapportionment.

30. The vice-president is the only elected officer who has duties in two branches of government. He or she serves in the executive and legislative branches.

31. Caucuses of the major parties in Congress originally chose the list of major-party candidates that the electors voted on for president and vice-president. Party conventions made up of delegates selected through political primaries and caucuses now choose the major-party candidates for president and vice-president.

32. Andrew Johnson was the only president ever impeached by the House of Representatives. He was not convicted by the Senate.

33. Judicial review is the right of a court to decide whether or not laws conform to the Constitution. *Marbury vs. Madison* is important because it marked the first time that the Supreme Court declared a federal law unconstitutional. This established the principle of judicial review.

34. The South had its economic interests protected by these clauses. As part of one of the compromises agreed on during the writing of the Constitution, the South was granted these clauses to protect the interests of southern slaveholders.

35. After the Equal Rights Amendment was introduced in 1923, Congress and the American people debated it for many years. In 1972 Congress finally officially proposed the amendment. Congress also said that the amendment had to be ratified by 1979 to become part of the Constitution. The deadline was later extended to 1982. By the deadline, however, only 35 states had ratified the amendment. Ratification by 38 states was necessary to achieve the three-fourths majority stipulated in the Constitution. So the ERA proposal died without becoming part of the Constitution.

36. the Magna Carta

37. Student responses to this question will vary. One example they might use is the *Reynolds vs. United States* case of 1878. In this case the Supreme Court decided that the Mormon practice of polygamy was not protected by the First Amendment's guarantee of freedom of religion.

38. The election of 1800 led to Amendment 12. In that election, Thomas Jefferson was nominated for president by the Democratic-Republicans, who also nominated Aaron Burr for vice-president. At that time, the electors simply cast two votes, without specifying which person they wanted to be president and which they wanted to be vice-president. All of Jefferson's supporters also voted for Burr, and the two tied in the electoral college balloting. The House of Representatives was forced to decide the election. Amendment 12 was adopted to make it clear in each election who was running for president and who was running for vice-president.

39. Because a number of presidents have been incapacitated while in office, student responses will vary. Following are two examples. On July 2, 1881, President James Garfield was shot twice. He survived until September 19, but did not perform the everyday duties of the presidency. In October 1919 President Woodrow Wilson suffered two strokes, which left him incapacitated. He died on February 3, 1924. During the time Wilson was ill, his cabinet performed many of the presidential duties.

Kentucky and Virginia Resolutions

1. An alien is an inhabitant of a country who is a citizen of another country. Sedition is conduct or language that serves to incite rebellion against a government.

2. a. The states are the members of the compact described in this section.

   b. This section says that the state governments have all powers not delegated to the federal government.

   c. This section says that the federal government should not be the judge of the extent of its own powers because that would make it, not the Constitution, the measure of its powers.

3. a. This section says that "acts which assume to create, define, or punish crimes other than those enumerated in the Constitution . . . " are "altogether void and of no force."

   b. This section says that the power to create, define, and punish crimes other than those enumerated in the Constitution is reserved to the states.

4. a. This section protests the Sedition Act.

   b. The Tenth Amendment and the First Amendment are quoted to protest against this law.

5. The Alien Act is protested in Section IV.

6. Article I, Section 9, of the Constitution is used in this section to argue that the deportation of aliens is unconstitutional.

7. First, this section argues that imprisoning aliens without a trial goes against the Fifth Amendment. It also argues that this action goes against the Sixth Amendment. The section then contends that the Alien Act gives the president the power to judge who is protected by the laws, and that this power is granted in the Constitution only to courts of law.

8. Strict construction of the Constitution maintains that the federal government has only those powers expressly delegated to it in the Constitution. Loose construction maintains that the Constitution does not literally define the powers of the federal government, and that some of the federal government's powers are only implied in the Constitution. Section VII supports strict construction of the Constitution.

9. a. In the early part of this section, the authors of this document pledge their support to the Constitution and the federal union.

b. This phrase means that the fact that representatives have been elected and the people have confidence in them does not mean that the people should not closely watch out for their rights.

c. This section calls on the other states to express their views about the legality of the Alien and Sedition Acts.

10. According to the first two paragraphs of this document, Virginia supports the union, the federal government, and the Constitution.

11. a. The powers of the federal government derive from the compact between the states.

b. This "instrument" is the Constitution.

c. The states have the power to stop the federal government from a "deliberate, palpable, and dangerous exercise of other powers . . ."

12. The Alien and Sedition Acts are protested in this paragraph.

13. The last paragraph of this document calls on the other states to declare that the Alien and Sedition Acts are unconstitutional.

14. The following quotations show that both documents support the compact theory of government. The Kentucky Resolutions state that "the several States composing the United States of America, are not united on the principle of unlimited submission to their general government, but that by compact under the style and title of a Constitution for the United States and amendments thereto, they constituted a general government for special purposes . . ." The Virginia Resolutions state that "this Assembly doth explicitly and peremptorily declare that it views the powers of the Federal Government as resulting from the compact to which the states are parties, . . ."

15. According to both documents, the Constitution is the instrument that keeps the federal government in check.

16. According to both documents, the states have the power to decide whether or not a law is constitutional.

17. Thomas Jefferson wrote the Kentucky Resolutions. James Madison wrote the Virginia Resolutions.

18. The Alien Act authorized the president to expel "all such aliens as he shall judge dangerous to the peace and safety of the United States." The Sedition Act made it illegal to write, say, or print anything "false, scandalous, or malicious" against the government, the Congress, or the president.

19. The Alien and Sedition Acts expired before Thomas Jefferson became president, and he did not renew them.

20. The states' rights theory says that the states have the power to decide whether or not acts of Congress are constitutional. The South most favored the states' rights theory.